Animal Ark

Special two-in-one edition

Hedgehogs in the Hall
Badger in the Basement

LUCY DANIELS

Hedgehogs
—in the—
Hall

Illustrations by Shelagh McNicholas

**Hodder
Children's
Books**

a division of Hodder Headline plc

*This edition of Hedgehogs in the Hall and Badger in the Basement
first published in 1996*
ISBN   0 340 67310 9
**Special thanks to C. J. Hall, B. Vet. Med., M.R.C.V.S. for
reviewing the veterinary information contained in this book**

Hedgehogs in the Hall
Special thanks to Jenny Oldfield

Text Copyright © Ben M. Baglio 1994
Illustrations Copyright © Shelagh McNicholas 1994
Created by Ben M. Baglio, London W6 0HE

First published as a single volume in Great Britain in 1994
by Hodder Children's Books

A catalogue record for this book is available from the British Library.

Typeset by Avon Dataset Ltd, Bidford-on-Avon B50 4JH

Printed and bound in Great Britain by
Cox & Wyman Ltd, Reading, Berkshire

Hodder Children's Books
A division of Hodder Headline plc
338 Euston Road
London NW1 3BH

To Fiona Waters, who showed me my first
hedgehog.

One

'Watch out, you two!' Mr Hunter warned.

Mandy and James jumped well out of the way of the garden mower. James's dad had almost finished cutting the grass, a job he disliked. James had been helping by raking up leaves when Mandy arrived, and the two of them decided to join in the garden chores together. Autumn smells of wet earth and leaf mould drifted in the air. It would soon be Bonfire Night.

'Watch out!' Mr Hunter yelled again. He stomped past, carrying a heavy load of grass clippings for the compost heap.

James and Mandy followed him up the garden

with armfuls of brown leaves.

'Whoa!' he said. He sprinkled the grass on to the compost. 'Drop that lot over there!' He pointed with his garden fork to another corner, under a beech tree. Then he plunged the fork deep into the compost.

Mandy let the leaves fall in the damp shade of the beech tree. She glanced up and saw James's new neighbour, a girl of about eight, peering silently over the hedge at them. 'Hi!' she said, cheerfully brushing leaves off the front of her jumper. 'I'm Mandy Hope from Animal Ark.' She remembered that the little girl had already been into the surgery with her pet rabbit. It wasn't eating properly. The move to a new house must have upset it. 'How's your rabbit?' Mandy asked.

But the girl didn't answer. Instead, her pale, staring face with its huge, dark eyes and frame of dark, straight hair, bobbed down behind the hedge without even a smile.

'What did I say?' Mandy wondered.

James shook his head. 'Don't ask me. I asked her over to visit yesterday. Mum said I had to. She did the same thing to me – just stared and vanished!'

'Hmm.' Mandy frowned. The girl couldn't be

all bad. After all, they had something in common: they both had pet rabbits! 'What's her name?'

James finished piling up the leaves and brushed his hands against each other. 'Claire something. She's the new doctor's daughter. I don't know.' He lost interest and went to rake up more leaves.

'Good Lord!' A sudden shout went up from Mr Hunter over by the compost heap.

Mandy sprinted over. James's dad stood, garden fork poised in mid-air. James ran up the length of the lawn to see what the fuss was about.

'Look!' Mr Hunter jabbed downwards with his fork. A large, round bundle of leaves, straw and scraps of newspaper rolled slowly on to the edge of the lawn. 'It's moving!' Mr Hunter cried. 'It's moving all by itself!'

Mandy gasped. The bundle, about the size of a football, was in fact rocking and trundling forward of its own accord. 'Don't touch it!' she said. She pulled at James's sleeve.

'What is it?' he said.

'Shh!' Mandy held up her hand.

Even Mr Hunter lowered his voice. 'I just stuck my fork into the bottom of the heap there, and hey presto, out came this thing on the end of it!' he whispered. 'What on earth's happening?'

'I'm not sure. Wait a moment!' Mandy crouched down beside the moving ball. She was sure her father had shown her one like this before, only not quite so big. It was in a hedge in their own garden at Animal Ark. 'I think it's a hedgehog's nest! Look!'

And sure enough, a long snout emerged from the ball and sniffed the air, followed by two dark, bright eyes, a pair of small, furry ears and two front paws complete with five sharp claws. Half in, half out of its nest, the hedgehog blinked at the daylight.

Mr Hunter, who liked gardening because it gave him a break from his work in the insurance office, leaned on his garden fork for support. 'I could've put a spike straight through that little chap!' he said, breathing a sigh of relief.

'Hang on!' Mandy knelt on all fours. James crouched beside her. The hedgehog was scrambling free of the disturbed nest. Its plump little body squeezed out between a gap in the interwoven wall. It half fell, rolled into a spiky ball, then landed on firm ground. 'It's not a chap!' Mandy whispered. 'Look!'

Four more tiny, dark noses followed. Four more pairs of front feet. Four miniature balls covered in pale fawn spikes tumbled out of the nest on to the grass.

'It's a mother hedgehog!' Mandy cried. 'And her babies!'

Mr Hunter wiped his forehead with the sleeve of his sweater. 'A narrow escape!' he breathed. 'Are they all right?'

'I think so.' Mandy had recovered from her surprise. 'I think they must like compost heaps for their nurseries. Loads of maggots and worms and things to eat.'

'Yuck!' James shuddered. He watched the mother unroll herself; sniffing, snorting and puffing herself up to take on any enemy. The babies unrolled too and queued up behind her in single file.

'They don't like the daylight though,' Mandy said, worried again.

'What shall we do?' Mr Hunter asked. He bent down as if to shoo the mother hedgehog back into the compost heap.

'No, I don't think that's any good. We'd better leave them.' Mandy knew not to interfere with a mother and her babies. 'If the mother's still nursing the little ones and we get in the way now, she's likely to turn round and destroy them!' Mr

Hunter and James looked shocked.

'What, she'd kill her own young?' James said, open-mouthed.

Mandy nodded. 'Or else she'd just desert them. And that comes to the same thing. Without her, they'd soon die!'

Since Mr Hope had shown Mandy her first hedgehog's nest, she'd been reading a booklet on the little creatures, not guessing how soon it would come in useful.

The three humans squatted on the edge of the lawn as the hedgehog family sniffed and snuffled to get their bearings. James and Mr Hunter waited for Mandy to decide what to do.

'She's probably got another nest somewhere nearby. They usually have half a dozen or so. Let's wait for her to find a safe one.' She sounded confident, but Mandy knew these little creatures only came out at night. Daytime smells, sights and sounds could easily confuse them.

They waited. The mother hedgehog sniffed the misty air. Her eyesight was poor, but she made up for it with a sharp sense of smell, according to the booklet. Soon the mother set off, zigzagging up the lawn, her babies close behind. They headed for wide open space, in the opposite direction to the hedge, their natural home.

'They're lost!' James whispered.

Mandy nodded. 'Afraid so. It's the daylight that's throwing them off course, but there's nothing we can do. Except keep watch!'

'They're heading for the house!' Mr Hunter groaned.

The miniature procession didn't swerve or falter now. It headed down the side of the house, straight for the chrysanthemum tub outside the Hunters' front door. Mandy, James and Mr Hunter followed at a safe distance.

'Maybe she'll find out she's going the wrong way!' James said, trying to be positive. 'They sure move fast, don't they?' The little hedgehog family had covered one hundred metres of lawn in double-quick time. Now they scuttled in circles in the area of the Hunters' front door.

Then up they went on to the first stone step, heads raised, sniffing the air, even the little ones! And up again in bold procession, mother and four babies, up the next step into the Hunters' hallway!

'They've gone inside the house!' James breathed. 'They're in the hall!'

'Hedgehogs in the hall!' Mr Hunter gulped.

'They're all covered in fleas and things, aren't they? Your mother will have a fit!'

Mandy tried to hold him back while the hedgehogs realised their mistake. But Mr Hunter had panicked. 'Chrissie!' he yelled to his wife somewhere inside the house. The hedgehog procession halted, perhaps puzzled by the feel of the hall carpet, the smells of polish and air freshener.

'Ye-es!' Mrs Hunter sang out from the kitchen.

'Don't come into the hall!' Mr Hunter warned.

But of course, that's what she did! 'What do you mean, don't come into the hall?' she demanded, opening the glass panelled kitchen door.

There was a bouncing, scrambling, scrabbling noise behind her; a large animal sound.

'Blackie!' It was James's Labrador, and James was first to realise the dangers. He shot up the steps into the hall, past the family of refugee hedgehogs. He wanted to grab Blackie before the dog pushed past Mrs Hunter and bounded down the hallway. A black Labrador's soft nose was no match for an angry hedgehog's spines. James lunged for the dog – and missed!

'What on earth's going on?' Mrs Hunter demanded.

Mandy too shot up the steps into the hall, to stand between Blackie and the hedgehogs. 'Down, Blackie! Stay down!' she commanded.

But the dog took no notice. He'd spotted uninvited guests. It was too late to stop him. He took three bounds and crouched, nose to nose with the mother hedgehog!

'Blackie, don't!' James cried.

They stood helpless. The hedgehog tucked her nose under her and flexed her backbone. She turned into a ball of strong, sharp spikes;

thousands of them. The tiny babies followed suit.

The dog growled. He kept his nose to the ground and bared his teeth. He snapped and lunged. Then he leapt back, yelping and whining. He almost felled Mandy, who stood there in the hall, helpless. Blackie recoiled in pain and anger from the hedgehog's dangerous spikes.

As the dog howled and retreated into the kitchen, the hedgehog made her getaway. Instantly she unrolled and was back on her feet. She was down the hallway before Mandy had time to think. Someone had already locked the wounded Blackie in the kitchen and the four little hedgehogs remained curled up on the carpet. They were probably petrified! But the mother was off!

Out of the house, past James's puzzled cat, Eric, down the steps, along the front path, scuttling at top speed!

'Stop her!' Mandy shouted at Mr Hunter. He stood astride the path between hedgehog and freedom. 'She's heading for the road! Stop her!'

'How?' Mr Hunter looked bewildered. Like Mandy, he thought too slowly to act. The hedgehog dashed past.

Mandy watched the terrified creature bolt for

the gate. She glanced down at the four babies, still tightly rolled and frozen to the spot in the Hunters' hallway. Then she ran after the mother.

The hedgehog had reached the garden gate. It was closed, but she shot straight under it. Too frightened to sense danger, she ran out into the road.

Mandy could hear a car coming. She flung open the gate. There was a screech of brakes. She heard it and couldn't bear to look. One hand went up to her eyes. The mother hedgehog had fled out of the Hunters' garden, straight under the wheels of a car!

Two

The accident was so sudden and quick that it was over before Mandy really knew what had happened.

The car brakes screeched and skidded. The engine cut out. Then silence!

Mandy uncovered her eyes. 'Let her be all right!' she breathed. 'Oh, please let her be alive!'

The car was slewed sideways, its nose pointed into the ditch on the far side of the road. It had stayed upright and in one piece, however. It was a big, silver car with mud spattered all along its side from the skid. A man opened the driver's door and stepped out on to the road. He was shaking his head.

'Did I hit it?' he asked anxiously. He was a tall, dark-haired man in a dark grey suit.

'I don't know!' Mandy cried. 'Where is she? I can't see her!' She looked wildly up and down the stretch of road.

'There!' The man pointed to the gutter by Mandy's feet. He pronounced the 'r' with a long Scottish roll.

Her heart sank. The hedgehog hadn't escaped the car wheels. She bent down to look, expecting the worst.

The mother hedgehog was curled in a tight ball, but one dark leg stuck out straight at an odd angle. There was no sound from the small creature.

'Oh!' Mandy half sobbed. 'She's hurt!'

'But alive,' the man said, bending down alongside Mandy. 'Her leg's broken, I think.',

'Poor thing!' Mandy exclaimed in a quiet voice. She looked down at the victim and began to get her thoughts in order. She was over the shock. Now she hoped she could save the hedgehog, and there was lots to do.

She went back to fetch the thick leather

gardening gloves which Mr Hunter always had stuffed into his waistcoat pocket, then she thrust her hands deep inside. 'There,' she said, gently beginning to talk as she rescued the hedgehog from the gutter. 'There, there, we'll look after you!' Slowly she slid a gloved hand under the tight ball. 'I want to get her away from the road,' she told the man. Gently she lifted the hedgehog, rocking her in the palm of the glove as she did so.

The man looked at Mandy and nodded. 'I'll straighten up my car,' he said. 'In fact, I'll drive it into my driveway. I live just next door. You can follow me!'

Mandy looked surprised. 'Next door?' In the house with the unfriendly girl?

He had one leg inside the car, one hand on the steering wheel. 'Yes, I'm a doctor. And you seem to know about animals. Between us we should be able to manage this!' He smiled, then he eased the car straight on the road. He drove it slowly down his own drive.

Mandy continued to think quickly. She glanced up the path to the Hunters' house. They were still inside, probably looking after poor Blackie and the baby hedgehogs. It would be better if she went with the doctor to his house to tend to the injured mother. She ran carefully down next door's drive, cradling the hedgehog in the giant gloves.

The same dark haired girl as before appeared silently from behind a pile of wood for the bonfire she was building at the bottom of the garden. Her father waved briefly at her but she didn't wave back. When she saw Mandy running anxiously into the house after him, she just stared and withdrew again into the shadow of the huge stack of wood.

'Quick, come into the kitchen. My wife's here. She'll be able to help,' the doctor said.

'I've run over a hedgehog,' he explained to the small, sandy-haired woman who met them at the kitchen door. 'Would you boil some water for us and fill a hot-water bottle? Then wrap it in a towel. The hedgehog's suffering from shock, so we've got to keep up its body heat!' He moved quickly, spreading clean tea towels on the table. 'Now,' he said, 'how do we unroll the poor wee thing?'

'I know how!' Mandy told him. She liked this man; his promptness, his Scottish accent. 'I live at Animal Ark,' she explained. 'My mum and dad are both vets. I'm Mandy Hope.'

'And I'm David McKay,' he said, shaking her free hand. 'Now I'll fetch the disinfectant from our first-aid box, in case there's any wound to wash down, while you have a go at unrolling her, OK?'

Mandy knew from Simon, the nurse at Animal Ark, that if you rocked a hedgehog gently back and forth, the movement would gradually make it unflex its spine. She began rocking, talking softly, while Mrs McKay came up with the wrapped hot-water bottle. Slowly the hedgehog let itself unroll, revealing a soft, browny-grey belly and one back leg completely dislocated. It still stuck out at an odd angle, broken and useless. Halfway down the dark leg, well above the little clawed foot, was an open red wound.

'Hmm . . .' Dr McKay frowned. 'We'd best bathe that with the warm disinfectant.' He gave Mandy a swab of cotton-wool dipped in the diluted mixture. 'I'll sort out a shot of antibiotic for her. Back in a tick.'

His wife stood by and watched as Mandy gently bathed and cleansed the wound. The little hedgehog sniffed and trembled, but didn't roll back up into a spiky ball. She let Mandy treat the injury.

Then Dr McKay came back and skilfully injected a small dose of antibiotic. 'Lucky, really,' he said. 'If you have to be a hedgehog who's run over, who better to rescue you than a vet's daughter?' He smiled at Mandy.

'Here's a nice, deep cardboard box,' Mrs McKay said, fishing for one in a cupboard under the sink. She put the hot-water bottle in it, amongst some loose newspaper scrunched up in the bottom. 'Now what still needs to be done?'

The wound seemed clean at last. Mandy discarded the cotton-wool swab and lowered the mother hedgehog into the warm nest. 'I need to take her back to Animal Ark,' she said, 'so we can set the broken bone.' She looked gratefully at Dr and Mrs McKay. 'I'd better go and let the Hunters know.' She picked up the box with the hedgehog nestled comfortably inside. Then another thought struck her.

'The babies!' She had last seen them in the Hunters' hallway. 'And Blackie! I'd better go!' Hurriedly she went to the front door. 'Thanks! I'm sorry I have to rush!'

Dr McKay nodded in his brisk, busy way. 'Not at all. I'm only sorry I was the cause of all this. I'll have to take more care in future!'

'I'm glad you swerved,' Mandy told him. 'Lots of people wouldn't have bothered.' She gave him a quick smile and went off down the drive. Then she nipped quickly back up the path to the Hunters' house.

'James!' she called. 'Is Blackie OK?' She stood on the doorstep with her cardboard box, anxious to keep the hedgehog out of harm's way.

James came out, slightly pale, but calm. He nodded. 'He's OK now. His nose bled like mad at first, but my mum washed it all off and disinfected it.'

'And the baby hedgehogs? What about them?'

James shook his head. 'I don't know. I'm sorry; we were so busy with Blackie I forgot to check,' he admitted.

Mandy looked down the empty hallway, then scanned the garden and down the side of the house. The babies had vanished.

'They're too small to manage alone!' she told James. 'They need their mother!'

'But you said the mother wouldn't have anything to do with them now!' James had come out into the garden to join in the search. He looked behind the flower-tub and along the lawn.

'Not if we have to handle them,' Mandy agreed. Then she had an idea. 'Look after the mother, will you, please?' she asked James. She handed the box to him. 'Her leg's broken. I've got to get her to Animal Ark.' But first she sprinted to the far hedge to pick up the empty hedgehog nest still lying by the compost heap. 'If we find the babies, maybe we can get them to crawl back in here,' she explained.

'Now what?' Mr Hunter peered out of the kitchen, one hand firmly on Blackie's collar. He'd taken off his gardening boots and stood there in big woollen socks. 'How's the other patient?' He pointed to the box. 'Still alive?'

Mandy nodded and explained again. But they were losing precious time. 'It's the babies we're worried about now. Do you know what happened to them, Mr Hunter?'

He thought for a few moments. 'Now, let's see. They were last seen in the hall here; four little spiky balls. One whimpering dog in the kitchen causing much chaos.' He scratched his head. 'Oh, now I remember! The four little balls unrolled, headed straight for the fresh air, after their mother. Didn't go off down the path kamikaze style like Mum, though. No, I think they took a sharp left by the flower-tub. They headed back where they came from!'

Mandy nodded. 'Thanks!' She scouted off down the side of the house, calling and peering under every bush. Under her arm she held the closely woven nest of twigs and leaves. She stooped low, studied the ground beneath the hedge, trying to find anything that looked like hedgehog runs. These were the tracks they wore through grass and leaves during their regular nightly visits. They were a sure sign of hedgehogs in any garden.

But she came face to face not with hedge-hogs, but with the McKay girl. Again! The pale face stared back at her from ground level. Mandy stared back at the serious blank face. 'Do you know where the baby hedgehogs went?' she whispered.

The girl nodded slowly.

'Where?' Mandy gasped.

'They're in my bonfire!' she announced. She said 'my' defiantly. 'They ran in there to hide!'

Mandy nodded. Of course; it was another good

place for hedgehogs, full of insects and beetles! 'Wait there!' she said. She had to be careful not to upset Claire. 'I'll bring their nest round and try and coax them out again. But don't touch them, OK? Just keep an eye on them!' She knew how vital it was to get the mother and babies back together without putting the scent of humans on them.

The girl vanished from the other side of the hedge, her face still pale and sulky.

'Remember, don't touch the babies!' Mandy repeated. She scrambled to her feet, grabbed the empty nest from the Hunters' lawn and sprinted along the length of the hedge to the front gate. She was up into the lane and down the McKays' drive, carrying the empty nest.

She headed for the half-built bonfire, making plans to rescue the whole family and take it back to Animal Ark. They would be able to look after them all and keep them with the mother. Mandy had it all worked out. She would coax the babies back into the nest with fresh worms or some other tasty morsel. They would be hungry. She hoped they would fall for her trick.

She ran as fast as she could. But it was already too late.

Claire stood there guarding her woodpile. She was holding a shallow plastic laundry basket. She held it up as Mandy arrived. 'I rescued them!' she announced, shoving the basket under Mandy's nose. 'I grabbed them before they could burrow further into the bonfire, see!'

Mandy looked into the basket. Inside the bare, white plastic container four little hedgehogs scrabbled and fought to escape. Their claws slipped on the shiny surface. They cried and called out in panic.

Mandy closed her eyes and groaned. 'I said, don't touch them!' she sighed.

Claire stared back, hugging the basket close to her body. 'You can't tell me what to do!' she retorted. 'They're not yours!'

Inside the basket the babies slid and squealed. 'No, of course they're not,' Mandy agreed, taking a deep breath. 'But they needed their mother!' She looked desperately at the girl. 'And now they need some proper extra care. We'll have to hand rear them!' It wasn't as good as she'd hoped for, but it was the best she could do. 'Please give them to me!' She put down the useless nest and held out her hands.

Claire stared back from beneath her dark fringe. Something wicked seemed to have got hold of her. She kept the basket clutched close to her. 'They're mine!' she said. 'I can look after them!' And swiftly she turned on her heel, and headed across the lawn towards the wide-open garage doors.

Mandy stood speechless. She watched the girl disappear into the garage with the four distressed babies. Claire had snatched them from their mother! She'd just turned all four of them into orphans!

Tears of anger stung her eyes as slowly she made her way back on to the road. James was there, silently watching. He handed over the mother hedgehog in her temporary bed without a word.

'I'd better get her home as soon as possible,' Mandy said quietly. 'Did you see what happened?'

James nodded. 'I'll keep an eye on her,' he promised. 'Try not to worry.'

Mandy swallowed hard. She set off up the road into the village, carrying her patient with great care. Her heart felt heavy and her eyes were still hot with unshed tears when she reached her own gate and the wooden sign

swinging in the breeze. 'Animal Ark, Veterinary Surgeon,' it said.

At least one hedgehog had reached safety, she
told herself. She would have to be content with
that.

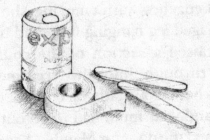

Three

'What have we here?' Jean Knox, the receptionist at Animal Ark, asked from behind her desk. 'Fish or fowl?'

Mandy gave her a weak smile. 'Neither. It's a hedgehog.' She set the box down on Jean's desk. 'Her leg's broken. We'll have to set it.'

Jean put on her glasses, which hung on a chain round her neck, and peered into the box. She noticed the hot-water bottle. 'I see you've already given her some first-aid.' She looked closely at Mandy. 'What's wrong? You seem upset.'

Mandy shook her head. 'Nothing. Who's on duty?' she asked. 'I'd like to get her seen to straight away. The poor thing's in pain.' The mother hedgehog wasn't moving; she lay quietly, her damaged leg hanging limp and useless.

Jean raised a section of the counter to let Mandy through into the treatment room. 'Simon's here. Your father's out at a conference in York and your mum had to go out on a call.' She opened the door for Mandy. 'A road accident victim by the look of things,' she told Simon. And she closed the door softly.

Simon was the nurse at Animal Ark. He'd only recently left college and still looked a bit like a student with his round glasses and serious face. But he was very good with animals, gentle and sure at the same time.

Mandy explained everything to him. She'd kept Mr Hunter's gardening gloves in a corner of the box. She used them now to cradle the hedgehog and lift it out.

Simon nodded. He never said much, but he took everything in. He gently examined the wound. 'Nicely cleaned up!' he said. 'Did you give her water and glucose at the doctor's house?'

Mandy shook her head and went quickly for the glucose solution. She knew it was to help the animal recover from shock. She'd seen Simon treat small accident victims many times before. Sometimes it was hedgehogs like this one, or else stoats and weasels caught in traps. She loved the careful way he handled these tiny creatures.

She watched as he dripped the liquid from a narrow tube into the side of the hedgehog's mouth. Then he turned back to the broken leg. 'Look,' he said. 'The bone's just pierced the skin here. But it's a clean break. No need to X-ray. He reached for a thin, perforated dressing. 'It's a simple fracture of the tibia. We can't use plaster of Paris straight away, just tape and a splint to hold the leg in place.

Efficiently, Mandy went for the tape and returned in time for Simon to fix the filmy wrapping into place with a sturdy strip of tape and plastic splints.

'Good,' Simon said, working quickly, with plenty of skill. Soon he had the injured back leg held firmly in place by stiff white splints. 'There, that should hold it still!' he said, standing back from the treatment table to admire their work.

Mandy couldn't help but smile at the forlorn little hedgehog with its stiff leg. She softly stroked its spines with her gloved hand. 'You look as if you've been in the wars!' she murmured.

'She has,' Simon agreed. 'But she should be fine now. And just to make sure . . .' He went across to another drawer, and with a flourish drew out a small drum of powder and a brush. He came back for one final treatment: 'A quick dust down with the anti-maggot powder!' he announced.

Even Mandy pulled a face,

'Nature's way!' Simon said brightly. 'Hedgehogs make wonderful homes for maggots, in-between those dangerous spines. And for fleas! Now the fleas are no problem; they won't jump off a hedgehog's back on to a human, so no worries! But maggots do carry infection, especially if there's a wound. It's nasty. So, lo and behold, one maggot-free hedgehog!' He finished dusting and once again he stood back from his patient. 'What will you call her?' he asked.

Mandy gazed at the sharp, knowing face, the inquisitive nose. She wanted a name that showed how hedgehogs roamed the countryside, little free spirits. 'Rosa!' she said. That was a gypsy name and it suited the little traveller. She scooped her up and back into the warm, home-made nest. 'What will she need to eat?'

'Toads, worms, caterpillars, earwigs, slugs,

dead mice, birds . . .' Simon reeled off a long list, then laughed at Mandy's horrified face. 'Or else cat food!' he suggested. 'That would be considered five star food by any hedgehog!'

'Phew, thank heavens!' Mandy said, with something more like her usual grin. Simon might look serious and studious with his short, fair hair and round-rimmed glasses, but he was always joking and teasing. 'What about bread and milk?' she asked.

'No, not really.' Simon cleared the table and disinfected it. 'Cows' milk contains bacteria which are bad for hedgehogs. I know people like to leave out dishes of milk for them, but I wouldn't recommend it myself. Water's better.' He wiped his hands dry on a paper towel.

Mandy nodded and made a mental note of everything. She was determined that Rosa would get the very best care.

'She'll be fine,' Simon reassured her again.

Mandy nodded. 'Thanks to you!'

'So what's the matter?' Simon asked gently. 'Why do you still look down in the dumps?'

Mandy stared down into Rosa's box. At last she brought herself to explain. 'Rosa's got four babies!' she said, shaking her head. 'I tried to rescue them too, but someone else decided they could do it better!'

'Who?' Simon asked quietly.

'Claire McKay!' Mandy spoke more loudly than she intended. And all her worries about the baby hedgehogs came tumbling out. 'They're so tiny!' she said.

Simon nodded. 'They're called piglets. I don't suppose they're weaned from their mother's milk yet, otherwise they wouldn't still be in the nest, would they?'

Mandy shook her head. 'So what will they do now?' she asked, desperation in her eyes.

Simon looked quickly at his watch. 'Well, we've finished surgery here,' he said. 'How about if we leave a message with Jean for your mother, and then I can come down with you to Claire's house?'

Mandy looked up at him with sudden hope. 'Would you?' she said. Her eyes brightened at the idea.

'Of course! Even if we can't persuade Claire to give us the piglets to look after, at least we can give her some good tips on hedgehog care!' Simon smiled and placed Rosa's box under the warm light of an incubator. 'It's worth a visit, wouldn't you say?'

Mandy felt a heavy weight beginning to lift. 'Why didn't I think of that?'

'Because you were worried stiff about four helpless little babies adrift in the wide world without their mother,' he said simply. 'It's understandable.'

Mandy nodded, smiled and heaved a huge sigh of relief.

So they set off together in Simon's battered old van. They rattled over the back lanes towards the road where the Hunters and the McKays lived.

Mandy rang the McKays' front doorbell with a trembling hand. She was glad Simon was standing there with her in the gathering dusk. She pulled her woollen scarf closer round her chin. They waited.

A light went on in the hall, then the door opened. Claire McKay stood, one hand raised and resting on the latch. She didn't speak.

'Hello!' Mandy tried to sound cheerful. 'There's good news about the mother hedgehog. She's going to be all right! We thought you'd like to know.'

Still there was no reaction from Claire.

'How are her babies?' Mandy asked. 'I've

brought Simon along just to check they're OK. Simon's the nurse at Animal Ark.'

Still no reply. Then Claire must have heard a movement behind her, from down the hallway. She moved as if to close the door. 'They're mine!' she said finally. 'No one else can look at them!'

'Claire!' Mrs McKay's light, soft voice floated down the hall. 'Who's at the door?' She sounded anxious, but she relaxed when she saw Mandy. 'Well, hello again!' she said to her. 'You must be freezing standing out there in the cold! Come on in!'

Claire scowled, but they accepted. If Mrs McKay could help keep Claire calm, Mandy realised they would have more chance of getting to the piglets. So, in the warmth of the kitchen, Mandy introduced Simon to Dr and Mrs McKay.

'How's the wee hedgehog?' Mrs McKay asked, offering them tea and special flat griddle scones with butter and jam.

'On the mend,' Simon said. He described Rosa's injuries.

Things were going well, Mandy thought. Everyone was friendly and concerned – except the dreadful Claire. She sat in a corner, angry and silent.

'Claire, why don't you take Mandy to see your

pet rabbit,' Dr McKay suggested after a long look in his daughter's direction. 'We'll finish our tea here.'

There was something clear and firm in his voice which even sulky Claire couldn't ignore. She stared back at him for a second, then turned and swung open a side door. It connected the house to the garage via a glass-roofed corridor which the McKays used as a laundry-room. Mandy peered through the door then looked back at Simon. He gave her an encouraging nod. 'You can sort her out,' he seemed to say. So Mandy followed the younger girl.

Claire squatted beside a wooden hutch. She lightly ran her forefinger along the netting and gave Mandy one sly, sideways glance. Then she set her face, blank and stubborn as ever, back towards the rabbit in its hutch.

'What's his name?' Mandy asked calmly. She watched the bright-eyed little black rabbit emerge from his sleeping quarters.

'Sooty,' Claire answered quietly, almost swallowing the word.

'Nice name,' Mandy said. 'I have some pet rabbits at Animal Ark. Do you want to come and see them?'

Claire ignored the invitation, so Mandy took a dandelion leaf from a small pile on the floor and held it against the netting of the cage. Sooty sniffed, came forward and nibbled warily. 'How old is he?'

'Six months. He was only three months old when we came. Now he's six!'

'And is he eating his food properly?'

Claire nodded. 'He likes it here now.'

'But you don't?' Mandy guessed. She thought she'd put her finger on something important. Still she had to be very careful with Claire. It was just like talking to a wild rabbit who would bolt at the first false move.

Claire shook her head. 'I liked my old house. And my old school!'

Mandy got close enough to Sooty to tickle his nose. She smiled. 'It takes a while to settle in,' she agreed. She remembered how nasty Susan Collins had been when she first moved into the area. All because she was unhappy that her mother had stayed in London to work.

'Everything's different!' Claire wailed. 'Nobody's my friend!'

'Is that why you want to look after Rosa's babies?' Mandy asked. She looked again at this strange, lonely girl. She wanted the baby hedgehogs to be 'hers' because she had no one to talk to, because she didn't fit in!

Claire blushed, nodded and ducked her head. 'Maybe,' she admitted.

'Well, will you let me be your friend?' Mandy asked.

Again Claire stared back without answering.

'At least let us help,' Mandy offered gently. The laundry-room was full of packing-cases and spare furniture. She looked round at all the chaos of moving house. But where was the side door into the garage? Although Mandy was beginning to feel sorry for Claire, she was still keen to get to those tiny babies.

Claire considered things carefully. She sighed. 'Simon knows all about hedgehogs; what they eat, how soon they can look after themselves, everything! He can help you take care of Rosa's babies!' Mandy said again.

Claire sighed one last time and stood up. 'OK,' she said. 'Tell him he can come and take a look!'

Mandy grinned, nodded and dashed back into the kitchen. She told Simon the good news. She saw Dr and Mrs McKay smile with relief, and some worry lifted from their faces too.

'I see!' Mrs McKay said. 'I've been wondering what's going on. So Claire's been looking after the hedgehog babies, has she!' She smiled at her daughter. 'She loves looking after animals of any kind, you know!'

Mandy smiled too. Now she began to regret having to tell them that they might have to take Rosa's babies away from Claire for their own good. She could see now just how much they might mean to Claire.

'She's been awfully unhappy since we moved from Edinburgh,' Dr McKay told Simon. 'Taking care of these baby hedgehogs could be just what she needs!'

Simon nodded. 'From what Mandy tells me, the piglets will be between four and six weeks old,' he told the McKays. 'If I can just take a look, I can advise you on what they eat, how often and so on.'

One step at a time, Mandy thought. *Let's just make sure they're still OK.*

Chairs scraped on the tiled kitchen floor as the three of them got up to follow Mandy through to the laundry-room. Mrs McKay switched on the garage light and Claire led them all into the chilly building.

She headed for the far corner, beyond her father's big silver car. 'I put their basket down by the side of the freezer,' she told Mandy. 'I put newspaper in so they wouldn't get cold.' Proudly she led the way.

Mandy felt Simon stiffen as he felt the cold. 'They'll need more than newspaper!' he whispered.

Squeezing by the car one at a time, they followed Claire to her makeshift nest.

'Oh!' Mandy heard her cry out in alarm. She was crouching over the white plastic basket.

Fear shot through her. 'What's wrong?' she cried.

Claire lifted scraps of newspaper. Her face had screwed up in panic, then the tears started. 'They've all gone!' she cried. 'There are none left!'

Mandy checked; urgently, quickly. She nodded at Simon. 'It's empty!'

'They've escaped. That basket's not deep enough. They'd be able to climb out in no time!' He too checked the empty nest.

Mrs McKay stooped to comfort Claire, but Mandy could only think of the four tiny hedgehogs. They were out alone, among the dangers of the real world! Foxes, badgers, and all the man-made traps of ponds, wire fences and busy roads lay in wait! Hunger threatened. They might get separated or lost. They could be dead already!

Mandy ran to the open garage door and stared out. Dusk had fallen; it was almost pitch black.

She looked desperately into the dark night, then ran into the middle of the McKays' lawn. She strained to see, to hear anything that might help. She listened intently.

And yes, amidst the rustling leaves she could hear another sound. A tiny, odd, pathetic sound that she remembered from earlier that afternoon. Her heart skipped and her mouth went dry. There was the sound again! It was the high, piping cry of tiny, lost hedgehogs!

Four

Mandy turned and looked at Simon, her face filled with dismay.

He joined her out on the dark lawn. 'Don't worry, we'll think of something!' he said, running one hand through his short hair.

The thought came to her in a flash. 'I know!' Mandy said. 'We could try and attract them back into the garden with a dish of food!'

'Good idea! Even though they're not completely weaned, they can still tuck into a dish of cat food!' Simon said. 'And we can ask the McKays if we can borrow thick gloves and a box to put them in. We'll be a sort of search party, up and down their hedges. A hedgehog patrol!'

'You ask for the box! I'll go next door for cat food, if Eric can spare it! Maybe James will come and help too!' Mandy forced herself to act. When she was doing something, she could push away those dreadful fears about the piglets' safety. She split off from Simon and ran next door.

James answered the doorbell with a peanut butter sandwich wedged in his mouth and a glass of Coke in one hand. His brown hair was tousled as usual, and his glasses were perched on the end of his nose.

'James, we need a dish of Eric's food to catch the baby hedgehogs! Don't ask!' she said, breathless and jumbled. 'One dish will do. And you can help if you want!'

Quickly James nodded, bolted his sandwich and raced to do as Mandy asked. 'Here's a torch!' He grabbed one from the kitchen drawer.

'And here's your jacket, James!' Mrs Hunter said. She flung it on to his back as he shot past. 'What is it this time?' she asked, confused by the search for cat food, a torch, and Mandy's breathless dash into the house.

'Operation Hedgehog!' Mandy said. 'We have to rescue Rosa's babies!'

'Oh,' Mrs Hunter said, going to the front door and holding it open. 'Rosa's babies. In that case I'd better hold on to Blackie!'

They tore down the hallway, out of the door, armed with the vital dish of food and the torch. 'Yes, please! Thanks, Mum!' James yelled back up the path.

Quickly they rejoined Simon on the McKays' lawn.

'It's OK,' Simon said. 'Dr McKay says search away. Mrs McKay's keeping Claire indoors though. She's upset enough already about the baby hedgehogs going missing!'

'I'll bet she is,' Mandy muttered. She remembered Claire's stubborn determination to 'rescue' the piglets. Being fond of animals was fine, but you also had to know what you were doing!

She set the dish of cat food on the grass. 'What now?'

Simon looked up into the night sky. The wind pushed great banks of dark clouds edged with silver across the face of the full moon. 'We wait,' he said. He pulled on woollen gloves and tied a scarf round his neck. 'Over here, out of sight.' And he led James and Mandy to the deeper shadows of the beech tree, where they squatted and began to wait.

Minutes passed and nothing happened. Only the mysterious night sounds interrupted their watch. A twig snapped in undergrowth beneath the hedge. A night bird, probably an owl, spread its wings in flight. And every now and then, the high, pleading call of the little hedgehogs crying for their mother broke the silence. 'Shh!' Simon warned. Still they waited.

'At least they haven't run away completely!' Mandy whispered. They were still circling the McKays' garden, calling and calling for their mother.

'Look!' James pointed across to the dark pyramid shape of Claire's bonfire. Something came out of the shadows.

'Too big,' Simon warned, holding Mandy back.

'It's Eric!' James cried. He'd recognised his own cat. 'He's heading for the dish of food, the cheeky thing!'

'Leave him,' Simon said. 'Just lie low and wait!'

They watched as Eric circled the dish. He stepped elegantly round it, dipped his nose towards it, raised his head, considered and turned away from the food. His ears twitched. A new sound had attracted him and off he padded, silent as a shadow.

James breathed out. 'He's just been fed,' he explained. 'Anyhow, he must have spotted something more interesting!'

They nodded.

'Shouldn't we move the dish nearer to the hedge?' Mandy suggested. 'In case the hedgehogs daren't come out into the open?'

'We could do that if we knew which hedge they were in,' Simon said. 'Their run could be anywhere, in any direction.'

Mandy nodded. 'Better leave it where it is, then.'

Still the wind chased clouds across the moon and dappled the garden with darker shadows. Still little animals rustled the grass and hopped through bushes unseen. But no baby hedgehogs appeared.

Cold almost to the bone, Mandy crouched in the shadows and shivered.

'Look, another visitor!' Simon pointed out.

This time it was an even larger, stealthier shadow than James's cat. It appeared out of nowhere, a sharp outline, still as a statue on the edge of the lawn. Then it moved precisely, menacingly forward. A white flash on its chest shone in the moonlight.

'It's a fox!' Mandy breathed. 'He's beautiful!' She saw his bright eyes glint and watched as he glided forward.

Without a second's pause he lowered his head to the dish and wolfed down the food. Then he trotted on. The brush of his tail swept the undergrowth of the hedge, and he was gone. Mandy held her breath in wonder.

Simon turned to James. 'Have you got more food at your place?' he asked.

James nodded, crept forward for the empty dish and hurried home to refill it.

'Don't give up,' Simon told Mandy. 'Those little ones can smell food from a long way off!'

'Unless that fox gets to them first,' she said, shivering again.

The new dish of food attracted many other visitors, but still not the invited guests. A tiny, sharp-nosed shrew sped across the lawn, snatched one bite and ran swiftly on. A huge stray tom-cat prowled down the drive, padding heavily towards the free meal on the grass. This time Simon stood up, jumped forward and waved his arms wildly.

He managed to scare off the old tom. 'All we need now is a badger!' he sighed as he settled back down.

'Shh!' Mandy's ears were tuned to every feeble baby hedgehog squeak. This one had sounded louder, nearer. And sure enough, a tiny round shape had stumbled out into the open. It stopped, gave a tiny snort and headed for the food dish! Mandy nearly cried out with relief.

'Wait!' Simon said steadily. 'Let him feed. The others might follow!'

Every bit of Mandy's body wanted to rush forward and rescue the piglet. But no; she waited, ready to move.

Bravely the hedgehog trotted up to the food. He put his two little front paws up against the side of the dish. He nosed the mashed meat this way and that, gave one final snort and began snuffling deep into the food!

'Let's call that one Scout!' Mandy suggested. After all he was the one who had boldly gone ahead and found the trail. And to her delight, another piglet emerged from the hedge; sniffing, zigzagging, following the leader. Soon he was snorting happily, his nose deep in the dish, his stumpy tail in the air.

'That's Spike!' James said.

Then came number three. Smallest of all so far, only seven or eight centimetres long, stretching to reach the dish, stumbling head first from the rim into the food and trudging happily into the very middle, up to her ears in it. 'Tiggy!' Mandy said. She looked up, bright-eyed with excitement, at the others.

'Where's the fourth one?' James whispered, staring deep into the darkest shadows of the hedge.

Mandy heard one last, forlorn piping noise. 'Here!' she said.

The last baby came forward, looking lost and lonely. But he'd heard the snorts and he'd smelt the tempting smell. With incredible speed he darted for the dish and joined the other three in hedgehog bliss.

'And that's Speedy!' James said with a grin.

'Ready?' Simon asked.

Mandy, James and Simon put on their leather gloves and crawled forward. They prayed that the little hedgehogs would be too busy feeding to notice them. They reached the spot. All four guzzled happily on.

'Now!' Simon said with a firm nod.

Mandy moved quick as a flash to scoop up Spike in her gloved hand. His face was covered in meat and he squealed in protest as she lifted him. She noticed a small patch of broken spines behind his left ear; this was how she would remember him. Swiftly she popped him into the box Simon had brought from the house.

James too had whisked a baby to safety. It was Scout, the one with the brave zigzag movements of the explorer and the careless, untidy air. Then Simon rescued tiny Tiggy and put her, protesting, into the box with the others.

'Watch out for Speedy!' Mandy cried. For the

fastest baby was making a quick getaway. The squeals of the rest had alarmed him; he was dashing for freedom again!

But Mandy half crawled, half ran across the lawn after him. In a sort of rugby tackle she managed to stop him just as he re-entered the run along the hedge. It was a rough capture, and Speedy squealed louder than the rest. But she had him safe and sound!

Mandy went back and popped the last piglet into the box.

James and Simon were grinning and slapping each other on the back. Simon gave Mandy a quick hug. 'Straight back to Animal Ark?' he asked.

She nodded. 'You'll come too, won't you?' she asked James.

'Try and stop me!' he grinned.

Together they knocked on the McKays' door to report their success. Then on to James's house with the news, before they all piled into Simon's van, tired but thrilled.

Simon flicked on the headlights as the engine coughed into life. 'See!' He pointed to two fully-grown hedgehogs trudging down the lane ahead of them. He shook his head and waited patiently for them to sidle off into the grassy bank. 'No wonder so many get killed!'

In a minute or two the road was clear. Then they were on their way through Welford, past the busy Fox and Goose, out again along the dark road leading to Animal Ark. Simon's van, rattly and uncomfortable, got them safely home at last.

Mandy saw her mother open the door at the sound of the van. She climbed out, carrying her precious refugees, and headed down the path towards Mrs Hope.

Mrs Hope welcomed them with a broad, warm smile. 'Come in all of you, close the door!' she said. 'Let's see what you've been up to this time!' She'd changed into trousers and a big, warm sweater, ready to relax after another busy day.

Mandy grinned back at her. She put the box on the scrubbed kitchen table, feeling the warmth of the stove. They were safe! Carefully she opened the lid.

Her mother peered in and murmured, 'Oh, well done!' She beckoned them all straight through to the surgery at the back of the house. The light was on. Mr Hope was in there checking Rosa's temperature. He hummed tunelessly as he worked. He looked up at Mandy with her cardboard box.

'She's fine,' he reported. 'Her leg's already on the mend. I should be able to put on the plaster dressing soon, when the swelling's gone down.' He stared curiously at the box. 'If I'm not mistaken, you're about to make this injured hedgehog's day!' he said.

Mandy nodded and came forward. 'We found the babies! All four of them!' She beamed up at him, showing him the four young ones curled up in the bottom of the box.

'This is Scout!' she said as she picked him up, skilful now in handling the hedgehogs. She put him gingerly in the warm incubator along with his mother. 'And this little one is Tiggy. This one's Speedy, and this is Spike!' Soon all four were in the clear cage with their mother.

'Now, let's see if she'll take to them again,' Mr Hope said. 'We might be lucky!'

Mandy peered anxiously into the incubator. The babies had been handled a lot since Rosa had made her own dash for freedom. Would she be happy to see them, or would she turn against them? Mandy held her breath.

At first Rosa squeaked with surprise. Then she

poked and licked and snuffled at each one in turn. She made little sideways moves, her clumsy stiff leg getting in everyone's way. Then she snorted with pleasure and shooed all her babies into one corner. They squeaked, struggled for position and grew breathless with excitement. She settled them down, bossing them with her snout.

Mandy looked up at the others in the surgery – Simon, James, her mother and father. She grinned. 'Back where they belong!' she said with a sigh.

She glanced down again, and there were four contented babies suckling, and one very happy mother hedgehog.

Five

'Animal Ark is really living up to its name!' Mrs Hope said early next morning. She watched as Mandy spooned out a dishful of fresh cat food for Rosa and her babies.

'I know, isn't it great!' Mandy agreed. Nothing felt better than rescuing animals and making sure they were safe and healthy. She placed the metal dish down in the hedgehogs' new home and watched them all tuck in.

'They've certainly got healthy appetites!' Mrs Hope laughed. 'Oops!' She watched as Rosa caught the smallest baby with her stiff leg and knocked her sideways into a bed of newspaper.

'Poor Tiggy!' Mandy laughed and set her back on her feet. 'She's a bit accident-prone!'

Mrs Hope leaned over Mandy's shoulder to watch the hedgehog antics. 'And when will it be safe to put them back into the wild?' she asked.

Mandy caught her bottom lip between her teeth. 'I don't know yet.' She'd thought of that question once, between leaping out of bed and brushing her teeth, but she'd pushed it to one side. 'We've only just rescued them,' she said. 'It's too soon to think about letting them go!'

'Yes, but you have to think about how to release them as soon as they're ready,' Mrs Hope insisted. 'All wild animals need to be set free. You know that!'

Mandy swallowed hard and nodded. 'I know.' It still wasn't something she wanted to talk about. She put down a dish of water and watched Rosa happily start to drink.

'Talk to Simon,' her mother said gently but firmly. 'He's the hedgehog expert!' And she went off to start surgery.

Mandy had ten minutes before she left for school. Ten minutes to do some very hard thinking! She gazed down at the baby hedgehogs. Already she loved this little hedgehog family. She knew each one by name and nature: brave Scout, the explorer; clumsy Tiggy; Speedy the sprinter; and Spike with the spines missing! She thought of Rosa the mother, and the nightmare of losing her babies. How could she, Mandy, bear to part with them?

Yet she recalled Claire McKay standing by her bonfire in the gloom, clutching the white basket of lost babies. 'They're mine!' Claire had shouted, sulky and mean. And in saying that, she'd almost ruined four little lives!

Of course, Claire had been upset when the babies vanished. Mandy remembered Mrs McKay rushing to comfort her. She'd cried as if the whole world had collapsed. But it had been wrong to put herself first and not think about the hedgehogs' welfare. Animals always came first with Mandy!

'I'm the same as Claire,' she told herself. 'If I say I want to keep Rosa and her babies, I'm just the same as Claire!'

So when Simon arrived to begin his day's work, Mandy had made up her mind. 'How long will it take us to get these hedgehogs fit and ready to go back?' she asked quietly. It seemed the hardest thing she'd ever said.

Simon gave her a quick, kind look. 'Back where they belong? A few days, a week at the most,' he said. 'I should say they're about five weeks old. At six they're generally ready to leave the nest and go their own way. Once their weight is up, we have to let them go straight away!'

Mandy nodded. A few days! That was hardly any time at all! 'And what do we have to do to help?'

'Feed them up. Weigh them every day. Once we get their weight up above four hundred grams or so, and once they're weaned from their mother's milk, they're ready to go!' Simon put on his white coat and buttoned it up. 'Shouldn't you be at school?' he asked.

'I'm on my way!' Mandy grabbed her school-bag and zipped up her jacket. 'In fact, I'm out of here!'

She was on her bike, up the lane and cycling like mad to meet James at McFarlane's post office. She didn't feel like talking as they rode over the moor to school. Sometimes caring for animals was hard and it hurt!

She plunged into her school day as if maths was the most interesting subject on earth. It wasn't, but it kept her mind off Rosa and her babies. Today she needed to leave Animal Ark behind and think of other things.

'Part of the problem,' Simon said that evening as he took Scout out of the cage for weighing, 'is the place they've chosen for their run.'

He put the hedgehog carefully on to the dish of some ordinary kitchen scales, but Scout snorted and scrambled straight out again. Simon scratched his head.

'You mean they're too close to the road?' Mandy asked. She scooped Scout up off the table and gave him back to Simon, who nodded. 'Once they've made a proper run, a track to follow, they stick to it?'

'Yes, because they build their nests along the route. It can be a couple of kilometres long, mind you.' Simon was developing another plan to weigh Scout. He took out a different sort of scale which worked on a spring balance, like a seesaw with hooks attached. 'Don't worry!' He grinned at Mandy as he saw her looking with alarm at the hooks. He began to make a sling from some fine white cotton fabric, and hung it from one hook.

'Two kilometres!' Mandy gasped. 'I thought

they just stayed around one garden!'

'No way. Hedgehogs are travellers.' Simon placed Scout carefully in the sling and began to balance the scale with weights. He concentrated hard. 'But Rosa's run is dangerous because it seems to cross the road just outside the Hunters' place. Three hundred and ten grams!' he announced cheerfully and noted it down.

Mandy held back a groan. Scout was a fat little hedgehog, doing really well on his new luxury diet of cat food.

'Do you think you can do this?' Simon asked.

She nodded and took over. Very carefully she

measured and recorded the weights of the three other piglets. None was as heavy as Scout, but all weighed in at around the three-hundred-gram mark, even Tiggy. 'What happens if they're too light?' Mandy asked.

'They won't be big enough to hibernate. Not enough body fat to carry them through the winter. Not to put too fine a point on it, they'd starve to death!' Simon had moved on to check a sickly white cockatoo with a bright yellow crest. It was new to Animal Ark and squawked moodily at Simon as he approached its cage.

'How come you know so much about hedgehogs?' Mandy asked, to change the subject. She still felt upset about letting go of Rosa and family so soon after she'd found them.

'I just like them,' he said. 'And I've a friend who did a special study on them. We were at college together. Now she works for radio, on the wildlife programme, *Wildlife Ways*. You know?' Simon chatted on. 'You'd be amazed by how much I don't know about them!' he insisted. 'Now Michelle; she's the real expert!'

They were interrupted in their work by a quick visit from James and Susan Collins. Susan was looking happier since she'd finally settled into the village. Prince, her pony, was fine too. Susan was in riding gear and looking radiant. 'Hi, Mandy! James says you just rescued some gorgeous little hedgehogs!' she said. 'Can I see them?'

Mandy left Susan cooing over them. She wanted to talk seriously to James. 'I'm wondering if we can reroute this hedgehog run,' she said. 'We don't want to put Rosa back in your garden and have her run straight out into the road again!'

James nodded thoughtfully. 'I'll think about it,' he said. 'But I don't know there's much we can do, short of digging a tunnel!'

Even Mandy agreed that was a bit too much to ask. She watched James and Susan leave together. As they crossed the surgery yard, they said hello to another familiar figure. Claire McKay had stepped out of her father's silver car and was heading straight for reception! Mandy's eyes widened. What did she want?

'Nearly home time,' Simon said. He glanced at his watch, then up at Mandy. 'Uh-oh, what's up now?'

Mandy's face had set into a frown and she pointed out of the window.

'Calm down,' Simon said. 'Let's see what she wants first.'

Claire came into reception alone. Mandy peered out curiously, then ducked back. Claire was carrying a blue shoe box with breathing holes poked into the lid. From inside the treatment room, Mandy heard her explaining to Jean. Jean murmured back. There was a pause, then Claire and the box were both shown in. 'Casualty!' Jean reported. She pointed at the shoe box, then she closed the door.

Claire hung back, her head bowed. Two straight curtains of dark hair slid forward to hide her face. Mandy suddenly thought she looked unhappy and very small.

'What have you got there?' Simon asked.

'Hedgehog,' Claire said in a faint voice. She shuffled forward and looked up at Mandy. 'I'm awfully sorry about the babies!' she said, her dark eyes full of tears. 'I never meant to harm them!'

Mandy saw how upset she was. 'You really care about them, don't you?'

Claire nodded. The tears brimmed over and began to trickle down her cheeks. 'I didn't mean to steal them!' she said.

And Mandy softened straight away. She could never hold a grudge against someone who loved animals. She went up to Claire smiling kindly. 'Never mind, they're all fine now! Is there something wrong with this one too?'

Claire nodded and opened the box without speaking. Mandy looked in on a well padded nest, warm and safe this time, with a full-sized hedgehog snuffling quietly in one corner. His back legs were all tangled in strong green plastic netting, the sort used by gardeners for supporting peas and beans. It seemed this old hedgehog had blundered into a heap of the stuff and managed to wrap it round his legs. Now he couldn't move.

'Where did you find him?' Mandy beckoned Simon across for a closer look. 'In the bottom of my bonfire,' Claire said. 'It's a good place for them, isn't it?'

Mandy nodded. 'Until we set it alight!' she warned.

'It's OK, I'll check it every day,' Claire promised. 'I've called him Guy!'

Mandy smiled, but Simon was snipping carefully at the tangled netting and looking slightly worried. 'What is it?' she asked.

'I'm not sure,' he said, freeing Guy and picking him up.

Mandy stood by Claire and waited for him to give his verdict. Claire began to tense up. 'He's OK, isn't he?' she said. 'His legs are OK now!'

'His legs are fine,' Simon said, setting the hedgehog down. 'But his eyes aren't, I'm afraid. Take a look!'

They watched as Guy turned in tight, slow circles on the table. Simon placed a pile of paper towels in his way and the hedgehog blundered into it.

'He's blind!' Mandy said slowly.

Simon nodded. 'Probably caused by an accident.'

Mandy looked closely and saw that the normally bright, beady hedgehog eyes were dull and blank. She heard Claire begin to sniff noisily again. 'Wait!' Mandy said. She went off for a dish of fresh food and put it down on the table, some way off from Guy. 'Watch this!'

Up went his nose. He snuffled the air, scented the food and headed straight for it, true as an arrow.

'Nothing wrong with his sense of smell!' Simon agreed. 'Maybe, just maybe . . .' He put a hand to his chin, deep in thought.

Mandy guessed what was coming next. 'Are you thinking what I'm thinking?' she said. 'He's blind but not helpless?'

'That's right. Hedgehogs rely on smell more than sight anyway. There's no reason he can't have a perfectly happy life as he is. As long as—'

'As long as someone looks after him!' Mandy leapt in. Her face was full of excitement. 'He needs someone special to look after him, to put out food for him and so on!' Both she and Simon stared at Claire.

'Me!' Claire gasped. 'Me! I'll look after Guy!' She dried her eyes. 'He can live in my garden, and I won't bother him, ever! I'll just put out his food and I'll keep an eye on him. That's right, isn't it?'

Mandy grinned. 'That's exactly right!'

'Oh!' Claire smiled and her face lit up. 'I can look after him! Wait while I tell my dad!' she cried. And she dashed out to fetch him.

Simon grinned at Mandy. 'That seems to have worked out fine,' he said.

Dr McKay came back looking puzzled but interested. Mandy explained carefully.

'Sounds like a good idea,' the doctor agreed.

'And just what Claire and Guy both need!' He thanked Mandy and Simon very much.

Simon described the shape and size of nest-box which might be useful for Guy to hibernate in. 'His blindness might prevent him from collecting materials for a nest of his own,' he explained.

Mandy took Claire off to show her how well Rosa and her family were doing after just one day at Animal Ark. Claire nodded and listened as Mandy explained the type of food Guy would like.

'He'll probably still forage for slugs and things. But the food you give him will help make up for what he can't catch; the things that move more quickly, like insects and millipedes.'

Claire nodded. 'OK. He'll have loads of room in my garden. I'll look after him,' she promised.

'Loads of room!' Mandy repeated. She recalled Claire's large garden and all the hedges and bushes and shady corners that hedgehogs liked. 'Yes, it's a good place for hedgehogs,' she said thoughtfully. Then an idea struck her. 'Listen!' She darted over to interrupt Simon and Dr McKay.

Simon glanced up. 'Hang on, Mandy's just had an idea, I can tell by her face!' he warned.

'I have! And it's brilliant!' she said. She could hardly keep still for excitement. She grinned at Claire.

'Well?' Dr McKay put his head to one side, smiling.

'Well, you have a huge garden . . .'

'Ye-es!'

'And Claire loves hedgehogs . . .'

'Aye!'

'And at the end of this week we have to put Rosa and Spike and Tiggy and Scout and Speedy back into their natural habitat!'

'Aye!' Dr McKay's voice rose higher and higher.

'And your huge garden is close to their run, so they would be able to find their way around right away!' Mandy said.

'If?' Dr McKay said cautiously.

'If you let us set up a hedgehog refuge in your garden!' Mandy said.

This was her brilliant idea. 'A sort of halfway house for Rosa and her family!' Mandy raced on. She was already thinking of special cages, fenced-in areas, feeding stations, lookout points. 'Please say yes!' she said. 'Just to help them get used to roaming free again!'

Dr McKay's eyebrows knitted then lifted. 'Like

a hostel for hedgehogs?' He began to nod and smile.

Claire was holding tight to his hand. 'Please, Daddy!' she cried.

Mandy knew how much this would mean to Claire as well as to her. Together they'd work on the problems of putting the baby hedgehogs back into the wild.

She stared into the doctor's eyes. 'We'll call it Rosa's Refuge!' she cried. She looked down at Rosa and her gorgeous family. 'Let's all work together to set them free!'

Six

'You realise we've got less than a week to set up this refuge!' Mandy told James. 'Simon says we have to let them go as soon as they're ready, so they can hibernate through the winter. The nights are already turning frosty!'

They'd just called in at McFarlane's to beg old, unsold newspapers to line hedgehog boxes. James was as keen as Mandy to get things organised. 'I'm just sorry it can't be in my garden,' he told Mandy.

Mandy slowed down and pulled her bike into the side of the road. Suddenly she saw that they'd chosen Claire's garden without talking to James.

He must be feeling left out. 'It's true, we couldn't have the hedgehogs at your place because of Blackie.'

James shrugged. 'I know.' His hair was damp from the drizzle. He seemed to be making an effort to cheer up though. 'Anyway, my dad and I have put extra wire netting along the hedge so Rosa and the rest can't just wander through. Blackie won't be able to bother them again!'

Mandy protested, 'It wasn't Blackie's fault!'

'And I'm racking my brains to see what else I can do!' James went on eagerly. He set off on his bike with a determined look. 'Come on,' he said. 'I thought you wanted to get to Ernie's place before tea!'

They rode quickly on and soon arrived at Ernie Bell's place. Mandy knew Ernie was the best carpenter in the area, even though he was retired. He'd built the fence for Lydia's goats up at High Cross, and he'd built it brilliantly. Now they were going to ask Ernie another favour.

'I made a quick drawing of an idea I had for a hedgehog's nest-box,' James said once they were inside Ernie's cottage. He took a piece of paper from his pocket and spread it flat on the kitchen table.

Mandy nodded. 'It's great, Ernie!' James was brilliant at measuring and drawing.

'We both think it should work OK,' James told Ernie. 'Look, it has to have a tunnel opening with a door you can lift . . .'

'The little tunnel entrance is to keep out badgers, see!' Mandy explained. 'The hedgehogs could even hibernate in here if you put a ventilation pipe in the top!' She pointed out various places on James's drawing.

'Steady on!' Ernie laughed and took his glasses out of his shirt pocket. He studied the paper. 'It's all measured in millimetres!' he said in disgust. 'Talk to me in inches and I might be able to manage it for you!'

'Does that mean yes?' Mandy asked. 'James says his dad has got spare wood in his garage and we'd be able to use that for the nest-boxes. We'll need five or six of them,' she said rapidly.

'Five or six!' Ernie stood back, hands on hips. He breathed out noisily. 'And I expect you want them all finished yesterday!' he grumbled.

'By the end of the week,' James said, his eyes hopeful.

Behind her back, Mandy had all her fingers

crossed. 'Of course, if you can't manage it, we'd understand!'

Ernie made a noise midway between a laugh and a cough. 'Nay, you've caught me out that way before!'

'Ernie!' Mandy pretended to be shocked. 'I've never caught you out!' But she knew that if she suggested one thing, Ernie was bound to do the opposite. It was the way he was. 'But really, I mean it; if it's too much trouble . . .' She picked up James's nest-box plan and began to fold it.

'Give it here!' Ernie said with a grin. He studied the drawing again. 'No problem,' he said. 'You can have six by the end of the week.' He pocketed the plan and tapped it to make sure it was safe.

Mandy gave a little hop of pleasure. 'Thanks, Ernie!' She turned to James. 'Come on, no time to be hanging about here! There's loads to do!'

James grinned. He insisted on looking in on Sammy, Ernie's tame squirrel, and on Tiddles the cat, curled up on the flowery sofa in Ernie's sitting-room. Then they said goodbye.

'And what's the name of this hedgehog hostel?' Ernie wanted to know. He stood in his shirt-sleeves at the gate.

'Rosa's Refuge!' Mandy told him.

Ernie gave a satisfied grunt and turned, ready to start work right away.

'Great!' James said as they rode off. 'I'm glad we live in Welford!' They set off back to his house to meet up with Claire. 'With people like Ernie around, we can really get things done!'

'And I'm glad you're looking more cheerful,' Mandy told him. Ernie had approved of James's plans. Now, like Claire, he was really part of Rosa's Refuge.

As they cycled out of the village, the light began to fade and an orange tinge had come into the sky. The hedgerows darkened to silhouettes. James snatched the time to tell Mandy his next idea. 'You know the problem you mentioned about the road? I've been thinking about it,' he said.

Mandy nodded. She loved the peace of these lanes, the feeling that small things went quietly about their business in the deep ditches and hedgerows while humans dashed madly by.

'Obviously we can't really dig a tunnel under the road for the hedgehogs,' James said. 'And I don't think we could train them to use a bridge! They'll have to keep on using the road as far as I can see. So what we have to do is make the cars slow down!'

'How?' She could tell when James had got stuck into an idea. His face went into a frown and he began to rush his words together.

'We make a sign!' James said. ' "Hedgehogs Crossing!" You know, like a "Children Crossing!" sign. It can be cows, ducks, anything!'

'Hedgehogs?' Mandy wondered. 'You mean a red triangle with a picture of a hedgehog?' Her eyes had lit up again. 'Do you think drivers would take any notice?'

'They would!' James insisted. 'If it were a good sign, properly painted, with a big notice underneath saying "Slow Down! Hedgehog Crossing!" Yes, it'd work!'

Mandy grinned. 'I think you're right!' she said.

'So shall we make the sign?'

'Yes!' Mandy attacked the next hill with new energy. Specially built nest-boxes, a proper sign, everything! Nothing was too good for Rosa and her babies. 'Let's go and tell Claire!' she said. She paused on the crest of the hill then freewheeled down. Things happened fast when you got involved in rescuing animals. Life rushed you along!

Dr McKay arrived home from work looking tired

and pale, but when he saw Claire helping Mandy and James to design the Hedgehogs Crossing sign at his own kitchen table, he drew up a chair to watch.

'Are we nearly ready for the grand opening? Is Rosa's Refuge going according to plan?' he asked.

All three of them nodded without looking up.

'And how long will these hedgehogs stay in your refuge?' Dr McKay took off his jacket and slung it around the back of the chair. 'I mean, how long before they're off on their own again?'

Mandy answered. 'Simon says it takes about three days for them to settle into their nests. Then we open up the doors and they're free to go!' Her voice trailed off at the picture of Rosa and the piglets wandering off into the night. 'We leave the boxes there though, in case they want to come back.'

'They will come back, won't they?' Claire asked in a worried voice.

'Oh, yes!' Mandy said. But she sounded more confident than she felt.

'Good!' Claire concentrated on her hedgehog drawing again. 'I wouldn't want them never to come back!' she said.

Dr McKay considered things as they worked and talked. 'So you'll need feeding stations? Places where you can leave food out without it being snaffled by any cheeky young cat, for instance?' He raised an eyebrow at James. He'd obviously heard of Eric's reputation. 'Don't worry about the cost of the food, by the way. I'll give you some money to cover that.'

'Thanks, Dr McKay!' James said. He grinned at Claire and Mandy.

'My idea is to put the dish of food at the centre of a loose coil of wire mesh. You fit a lid over the top. It's like a maze; you have to follow the path into the centre.' He drew them a quick pencil sketch. 'It's too small for cats, but wee hedgehogs have a knack of squeezing through narrow places, eh?' He paused to see what they thought.

'Brilliant!' Mandy said.

'Aye, well, I've been thinking of making such a thing for Guy in any case.' He smiled at his daughter. 'So maybe I'll just make a few more!'

Claire beamed up at her father. 'Do you like my drawing?' she asked. It was a big, bold black and white drawing of a hedgehog, all prickles, snout and feet. James was designing a red triangle, and the words, 'Slow Down! Hedgehogs

Crossing!' to fit underneath.

Dr McKay gave her a cuddle. 'Terrific!' he said.

'I think we'll be ready!' Mandy said. 'I can hardly believe it!' Each hour seemed to bring them closer to making life safer for Rosa and her babies.

But out at the gate, just where Rosa had had her accident, Mandy had another shaky reminder of the important job they had to do.

It was already dark, and Mr Hope had arrived to take Mandy home. She said goodbye to the others and put her bike into the back of the Land-rover. Then she climbed in. She was tired but pleased. They'd all worked hard on Rosa's Refuge and her father gave her a sympathetic grin. He switched on the headlights. Mandy waved at James and Claire then she faced forward, sinking deep into the comfortable seat.

Suddenly she shot forward. 'Oh, no!' She unclipped her seat-belt. 'Oh, Dad, look!'

There on the road, ten metres ahead, creeping along at snail's pace, snuffling and poking into the muddy puddles, was yet another young hedgehog! Mandy slipped quickly out of her seat, down on to the grass verge.

'Mind the road!' Mr Hope warned. He followed quickly.

Mandy went ahead. She saw clearly how so many hedgehogs managed to get themselves run over. This one didn't scuttle off sideways into the long grass at the blinding glare of lights. No, this hedgehog had simply stopped dead still and curled up in the very middle of the road! He was a sitting target!

'That's exactly the wrong thing to do!' Mandy told him. But how was he to know? She looked and listened for traffic. No cars were coming, thank heavens. 'Lend me your jacket, Dad,' she said urgently.

Mr Hope glanced down at his best leather jacket. He looked from it down at the hedgehog curled up still as a statue in the road. 'Oh no!' he said, putting two and two together. He made as if to zip up his jacket tight.

But Mandy insisted. 'Yours is good thick leather! Take it off quickly, Dad, please! There might be a car coming!'

She didn't have any gloves to protect her hands, so she waited while her father took off his jacket. Then she took it and wrapped it round her hands. Gently she rolled the hedgehog on to it. Once it was safely cradled in the leather jacket, she walked back towards James and Claire. 'We'll put it in the garden with a dish of food,' she said. 'Then it'll be safe.'

'Lucky it was you setting off down the road,' James said. He gave a hand with the food and soon the hedgehog was tucking happily into the free meal. 'One more hedgehog saved!' he added.

'One more accident waiting to happen!' Mandy sighed. 'I only hope your crossing sign works!'

At last they could set off home. Mandy was doing all she could, but life for the hedgehogs was still full of dangers.

Mandy was deep in thought as Mr Hope drove home. Tomorrow was the big day. Ernie's nest-boxes would be ready for collection, and James and Claire's sign could be put up by the road. Scout, Speedy, Tiggy and Spike were gaining twenty or thirty grams in weight each day. Rosa's leg was in plaster now, but she'd got so used to it that she could move on three legs almost as fast as Speedy on four! Nothing could get in the way. Rosa's Refuge was about to open!

She should feel happy and excited, she told herself. A hedgehog hostel was a great thing to be setting up. But she thought of Claire having to say goodbye to the babies if they decided to go off to new gardens, or new fields and hedgerows. Poor Claire had had so many goodbyes already this year, to her old house and her friends in Scotland. But perhaps tomorrow would be different, she told herself. Perhaps tomorrow, when it all actually happened, they would be glad!

'Don't you ever go home?' Mr Hope asked Simon. He was putting instruments into the sterilising unit.

It was teatime of the big day. Simon was giving Scout and the other young hedgehogs one last check over. 'Once in a while I do manage to call in there,' he grinned. He gave Mandy the figure for Scout's weight chart. 'Four hundred and five grams!' he announced.

Mandy wrote it down and sighed. 'They're ready!' she said.

'They are,' Simon agreed.

'Tonight's the night!' Mr Hope said.

'Tonight's the night!' the sick white cockatoo mimicked. He wagged his head sideways and danced on his perch.

'You're feeling better!' Mr Hope commented.

They all laughed. Mandy helped to lift Rosa and her family in their special cage into the back of Simon's van. She'd arranged to meet James and Claire at Rosa's Refuge at six. Dusk was already falling. It was a misty, still evening. Damp leaves squelched underfoot. 'It's all right, calm down,' Mandy whispered to Rosa. The hedgehog had raised her head to sniff at the old familiar garden smells from the safety of her cage. 'No need to worry. We're taking you home!'

Mandy's voice seemed to calm her and she settled back amidst the prickly heap of sleeping bodies.

'We have to call at Ernie's on the way, remember!' she said to Simon.

He nodded and started up the engine as Mandy climbed in.

'Good luck!' Mr Hope said, leaning against Mandy's open window. He gave her one of his lopsided grins.

'Thanks, Dad!'

She kept one wary eye on their passengers all the way down the bumpy road. She wished Simon's van wasn't quite so old and rattly. Outside the Fox and Goose, Simon pulled in. Mandy hopped out, down the side of the pub to the row of cottages where Ernie lived.

'Hello, Walter!' Mandy called out and waved to Walter Pickard, a neighbour of Ernie's who had a house full of cats. He waved back through the cosy square of lighted window.

Ernie was at his own door, waiting to greet her. 'I was beginning to think you'd got lost!' he grumbled.

'I said half past five!' Mandy protested.

'Aye, and it's twenty-five to six!' Ernie pointed out. He handed her a nest-box. 'Well, what's the verdict?' he asked.

Mandy looked at the beautifully made box, the size of a portable television, with a little tunnel entrance jutting out of the front and a piece of ventilator pipe sticking up from the roof. 'It's wonderful!' she said. 'It's absolutely wonderful!'

She and Simon helped him carry all six of the boxes into the van. No hedgehog could wish for better accommodation!

'And!' said Ernie on the last trip back to his cottage. 'I've made you a little something else!' He stood on his doorstep, hands in pockets, grinning.

'What is it?' Mandy asked.

Ernie leaned back behind the door and drew

out a wooden board cut into the shape of a house. It was a sign of some sort, with two short chains to hang it up. Ernie swung it in front of Mandy. Letters were etched into the wooden surface and stained dark brown. The board shone with clear varnish: 'Rosa's Refuge' the letters read, big and bold. Underneath was a row of five stars!

Mandy laughed. 'A five star hotel for hedgehogs!' she said with delight, and took the sign from Ernie. 'We'll hang it from a tree in Claire's garden!' she promised. 'So everyone will know!'

She felt very proud as they drove off, and her spirits soared.

In any case, when they arrived at Claire's house with the nest-boxes, the sign and the hedgehogs themselves, Mandy discovered there was no chance of keeping quiet about Rosa's Refuge.

'Who are all these people?' she asked Simon. She recognised Dr and Mrs McKay, Mr and Mrs Hunter, James and Claire. But in amongst the group were people she'd never seen before. One of them carried a camera over his shoulder.

'Ah, it's a surprise,' Simon said, studying his fingernails and pretending to look embarrassed. 'These are just some people I phoned and invited along to the grand opening!'

And that was all he had time to say before everyone came running up. 'Where are the hedgehogs?' someone asked. There was a buzz of excitement in the air.

'Could we have a picture of Mandy, James and Claire?' said the man with the camera.

'They're reporters!' James whispered, his face red and shiny. 'They heard about Rosa's Refuge. They want to put it in the local paper!'

'Oh, no!' Mandy gasped. She was hustled into the garden.

Ernie's shiny sign was hung from the beech tree. Then James and Claire had to hold up their own red triangle sign. 'A bit closer, that's right! Hold the sign up a bit, that's good! Now smile!' the photographer called as they stood in line. They smiled and the camera flashed. 'Great, thanks!' he said.

'Blame me,' Simon said to Mandy. 'I thought you deserved to have your names in the paper for this!'

Mandy had gone red from smiling into the camera, but the photographer gave way to another stranger. He asked lots of questions about how they'd rescued Rosa after her accident,

and how they'd helped her look after her babies. Mandy explained the idea of Rosa's Refuge. 'It'll be their pre-release place to stay, nice and safe, until they feel happy to explore and make their own nests again,' she said.

The fair-haired reporter began to write down her answers. 'Ready for winter?' he asked.

Mandy nodded. 'Yes, now's the time when they hibernate. We want them to lead normal hedgehog lives. They need every chance we can give them,' she said.

'And that's the idea of the "Hedgehogs Crossing" sign too?' The reporter sounded really interested. He was writing everything down.

Mandy nodded again. 'Can you put that in the paper, please? This road is a busy hedgehog run. We want cars to slow down and give way!' She tried to make sure that he told his readers that. 'It was James Hunter's idea! And Rosa's Refuge was thought up by Claire McKay and me! This is Claire's garden. We couldn't have done it without her!'

He wrote it down. 'Good! And now just one last question,' he said, pencil poised.

'Yes?' Mandy was keen now to get on with the real job of setting up the nest-boxes in good, secret corners of Claire's garden.

'Well, you've gone to all this trouble to save the hedgehogs' lives. Our readers will really admire you for that. But how will you know if it's worked? How will you know whether or not they've survived?'

Mandy let the question gradually sink in. 'We won't,' she said faintly.

He clicked his tongue. 'Pity,' he said. 'That would have made a perfect happy ending to the story!' Then he shut his notebook, thanked her very much and went off to collect his photographer. 'Look in next week's paper!' he called. They stood by their car, ready to leave. Then waving cheerfully, they drove off.

And then everyone had to lend a hand to get the nest-boxes into place. They chose shady places and disguised each one with twigs and leaves. Then they set up the doctor's wire mesh feeding stations. It was a busy, bustling time. Claire chose a special place for Guy's nest-box, close to the garden shed where she could keep an eye on him. Mandy made sure that all the tunnel entrances to the nest-boxes were clear.

It was all helped along by cups of tea from Mrs McKay. The lawn was criss-crossed by torchlight beams, wellington boots, voices calling. At last it was time to fetch Rosa, Scout, Spike, Tiggy and Speedy from the van. Mandy lifted their cage with great care and carried them over.

They held their breath as Mandy put on a pair of sturdy garden gloves and peered down into the cage. She chose Spike and picked him up first. 'Today's Friday!' she told him. 'If you stay in your new box for three days, on Monday we'll open your door and you'll be free to go!'

He grunted. Free to roam the hedgehog runs in gardens and fields, Mandy thought. Through hedges and into woodlands. He would be a wild hedgehog again!

Spike sniffed her glove and waggled his fat little body from side to side.

Mandy smiled fondly down, but she couldn't get Claire's worried look and the reporter's final question out of her mind! 'How will you know if they've survived?' he'd asked. And her own answer: 'We won't!'

She felt Claire smiling bravely at her. There was a catch in her own throat as she crouched down close to the ground with Spike. Mandy showed him the cosy box Ernie had made. 'We won't know,' she told herself. 'We won't ever know!'

Seven

Spike, Speedy, Tiggy, Scout and Rosa all moved without a hitch into their special nest-boxes in Rosa's Refuge. Claire was thrilled when she could bring Guy along to join them.

'You can leave his door open right away,' Simon told her. 'We know he can poke and potter around in the garden by himself. Are you feeding him up well for the winter?'

Claire nodded. She put the blind hedgehog into his smart new nest-box and sighed happily.

'Come and tell me if this is a good place for the road sign!' James called. He struggled with the large white triangle edged with red, showing

Claire's drawing of a hedgehog. At last he held it, shoulder high, against a fence post outside his garden.

Mandy went and stood a few metres down the road to judge the effect. 'That's great!' she said. 'Everyone can see that clearly!'

Then they had to go and make sure that all Rosa's family had enough food and bedding inside their boxes. For a moment Mandy stooped to peer in at one of them. She watched as Tiggy, still the smallest, dived into the middle of the messy heap of leaves and newspaper. Then Tiggy began turning round and round on the spot, using her spines to comb the nest lining into place. Soon she had a neat-looking, round nest. 'So that's how it's done!' Mandy said, impressed.

They all made one final check around Rosa's Refuge. They pegged the wire feeding stations into place with tent pegs and made sure each had a dish of food and one of water for any of the local wild hedgehogs who fancied a free supper. Rosa's Refuge was to be open to all.

'Ready?' Simon asked.

Mandy looked at Claire and nodded reluctantly.

'Come on then, let's go.' Simon blew warm breath on to his cold fingers. 'See you tomorrow!'

he said to James and the McKays. 'Come on, Mandy!' He stood by the van, stamping his feet.

'Don't worry,' Mandy told Claire. 'Everything's going according to plan!' She gazed around the garden. The nests were well hidden. The hedgehogs were safe inside. The 'Rosa's Refuge' sign swung slightly in the breeze. All was well.

She waved and jumped into the van without smiling. Simon drove carefully off.

'The "Hedgehogs Crossing" sign looks good; very easy to see!' he commented. 'Let's hope it works!'

Mandy just nodded. Simon headed for Welford.

'Do you want to tell me about what's worrying you and Claire?' he asked.

Mandy looked out at the cheerful, lively scene inside the Fox and Goose. People were chatting, drinking and having a good time. Somehow, it made her feel worse. She glanced at Simon's thin, serious face. His glasses winked and shone under the street lamps. Perhaps he would understand why they still felt low.

'I know Rosa's Refuge is a great success,' she sighed, 'and everyone has worked really hard on it . . .'

'But?' Simon prompted. He signalled and turned up the lane to Mandy's house.

'But Claire and I feel the same way. We want the hedgehogs to stay in Rosa's Refuge. Otherwise we won't know what happens to them,' she confessed. 'I can stand having to let them go. But I can't stand not knowing if they're alive or dead!' Her lips trembled as she spoke.

Simon nodded. He steered up the lane to Animal Ark.

'I know; you're going to tell me that's just the way it is,' Mandy said miserably. 'There's nothing we can do to keep track of hedgehogs once they're set free!' She tucked her chin into her warm scarf and screwed up her face to fight back the tears.

But she was mistaken. 'Keep track, you say?' Simon said slowly. 'Is that what's been bothering you two?'

'Yes. Claire says she'll have nightmares about foxes and cars and badgers and . . .' She could run on endlessly through all the disasters Scout or Tiggy might meet.

'I see!' Simon said. He slowed down and stopped at the gate of Animal Ark. 'Keeping track!' he said again. He waited until Mandy had climbed out of the van and watched as she used her key to unlock the front door. Mrs Hope was hovering in the hall. 'Mandy!' he called.

'Yes?' She came running back to meet him, curious about the new tone in his voice.

'Listen, I can't promise anything!' he said quickly. 'But I've had an idea. I want you to come down to my place around lunch-time tomorrow, OK?'

'Why?' she said.

'Can't tell you yet. I'll tell you tomorrow!' he said, looking excited and secretive. And he drove off without another word.

'How did the grand opening go last night?' Mr Hope yawned over his morning newspaper.

Mandy gulped down her orange juice. 'Fine!' She was already looking at her watch. The gap between breakfast and lunch seemed endless. What was Simon's secret? She had to wait another five hours before she found out.

'Your mother tells me you're going to be famous!' her father said. His mouth twitched into a smile. 'Rosa's Refuge is going to be in the newspaper!'

Mandy pulled a face. 'It's all Simon's fault! He

invited all those people from Walton!'

Mr Hope grinned. 'He's very proud of what you and James and Claire have done for those hedgehogs!'

Mandy felt a warm glow of pleasure. 'Hmm. They say it'll be in the paper next week. Now I have to go and check on Rosa and company!' she said, jumping up and grabbing her jacket. 'And then I'm off to Simon's flat!' As usual, she was already halfway out of the door before she'd finished speaking.

Rosa's Refuge looked calm in the crisp morning light. Mandy had called on James and Claire, and together they trudged through banks of fallen leaves to check the empty dishes in the feeding stations. Then they looked over the six nest-boxes to make sure they hadn't been disturbed. Everything seemed fine.

But Mandy felt Claire tug at her sleeve and whisper something in a worried voice. 'Mandy, you do think they'll come home, don't you?' she said again. 'I mean, Guy comes home every morning, so Rosa and her babies will too!'

'We don't know that for sure,' Mandy had to remind her gently. 'The important thing is to make it safe for them to go free again. That's why we've set up Rosa's Refuge, remember!'

'But I don't want them to go away!' Claire said in a trembling voice.

'Nobody does,' James said quietly.

Mandy looked at Claire. 'I think Simon's got an idea that might help,' she told her. She couldn't bear it when Claire looked so unhappy. 'But we have to wait until lunch-time before he tells me what it is.'

Claire looked up and nodded bravely. 'OK,' she said. She did seem suddenly happier, as if Mandy could sort out the whole world's problems.

Mandy only wished she could! She and James filled the rest of the morning by taking Blackie for a long walk into the woods behind James's house. They watched the black Labrador race through the trees after a stick. He skidded down slopes to fetch it and charged back breathless and delighted. At least it kept their minds off Simon's secret.

'Good boy, Blackie, good boy!' James said. Mandy patted his flank, glad that he'd recovered from the hedgehog attack.

'Time to go!' James decided at last. They led Blackie back home. Mandy left him with James and cycled into Walton. It was almost lunch-time!

She propped her bike against the stone gatepost of Simon's house. He lived in the ground floor flat of a big old house, in a room cluttered with empty cups, old wildlife magazines and a full set of drums. She knocked on the heavy green door and waited. Simon opened it and greeted her with mock surprise. 'Mandy!' Then he broke down into a grin. 'So you didn't forget?'

'As if!' Mandy walked past him into his room. It was messy as usual, but there was a woman sitting in the single battered armchair. She stood up when Mandy went in.

'Mandy, I'd like you to meet Michelle Holmes. Remember, I told you about her? She's the real hedgehog expert!' Simon introduced them.

'You work for *Wildlife Ways!*' Mandy said, thrilled to meet Michelle. She was a small, dark woman with short dark hair and big silver earrings, dressed in practical black trousers and a thick crimson sweater. But what was she doing here, Mandy wondered. Was she part of Simon's secret?

Michelle smiled at Mandy and picked up her mug of coffee from the mantelpiece. 'Simon's been telling me about your great work at Rosa's Refuge!' she said. 'It's one of the best projects

I've heard about for quite a while!'

Mandy nodded and waited. She felt there was more to come. What was Simon up to? He stood rocking his feet against the tiled fireplace, looking innocent.

'He was telling me that you want to set up a tracking system for your hedgehogs, once you release them into the wild?'

Mandy's heart jumped. 'Yes!' she cried. 'But how do you track a hedgehog through all those dark little runs? You can't even see them, let alone tell which one's which! Anyway, I don't see how you can!' she admitted.

Michelle nodded. 'It's hard. But I've been thinking about it for our programme. It's all to do with tiny radio transmitters that send out a special signal for each animal.' She sounded excited as she described her idea to Mandy. 'You fix the transmitter to your fox, or your badger or your hedgehog – whatever – with a tiny sterile pin. It's a bit like piercing the base of the ear, really. The pin has a small tag which glows in the dark. And it has a radio signal which we receive on this hand-held receiver.'

Michelle took something like a mobile phone out of a shoulder bag and placed it on Simon's table. 'The signal can be picked up from a distance of one kilometre and it gets louder as you get nearer to the transmitter – just right for your little hedgehogs' nightly rambles!'

Mandy took a deep breath. 'It's brilliant!' she said, still hardly daring to hope.

'Simon rang me last night and told me about your plans to set your hedgehogs free,' Michelle went on. 'He said you were keen to track them, and of course I said, "Look no further!" ' She paused and smiled. 'Would you let me try out my transmitters on Rosa and her family for *Wildlife Ways?*' she asked.

Mandy closed her eyes. Had she heard this right? Was it true? She opened them again. 'When?' she asked breathlessly.

'When will you be ready to start?'

'Monday!' Mandy told her.

'Monday it is!' Michelle agreed.

After that Mandy sailed through the weekend. She was brimming full of excitement.

She rang James and Claire right away to tell them the good news. Claire was thrilled. 'Does that mean we can follow them wherever they go?' she asked.

'Yes, it means we won't lose them once we set them free!'

There was a pause, then Claire said, 'You're great, Mandy! You're the best friend anyone could ever have!' Then she put the phone down in a rush.

Mandy sighed happily. She thought of Claire when they'd first met; moody and pale, lonely and frightened. It was all changed now, thanks to Operation Hedgehog!

She went away and bubbled over with the news to everyone she met.

'We're going to track the hedgehogs!' she told her grandparents when they came to tea on Saturday. 'We'll be able to track exactly where they are with a radio transmitter!'

Her grandfather thought that the technology was wonderful. 'They never had anything like that in my day!' he said.

'And what a thrill to be on *Wildlife Ways*!' Gran said. 'I always listen to that!'

Mandy sat cross-legged on the sofa, totally happy.

'I wish it was Monday!' she said to James and Claire on Sunday at teatime. They were checking the hedgehog nests at dusk as usual, and saying hello to Guy. 'We'll be able to do the tracking each dawn and dusk until we're sure everyone's OK. Will you be able to come too?'

James nodded. 'I've told my mum and dad it's a scientific experiment,' he said.

'It is!' Mandy insisted. 'And it's the first of its kind!' She felt very important, and honoured that Michelle had chosen them.

Claire followed them round, her face lit up with silent excitement. But as Mandy got ready to leave, Claire took her to a quiet spot under the beech tree. 'I don't mind at all now!' she announced bravely.

Mandy smiled. Claire sometimes said things in a funny, old-fashioned way that made her sound older than eight. 'What don't you mind?' she said.

'Having to let them go! As long as we know where they are, I'll be perfectly happy!'

'Me too.' Mandy gave her a quick hug.

'We do have to let them go, don't we?' Claire said quickly.

'We do.' Mandy was suddenly serious. Claire was learning a lot about letting things go. They'd help each other to get over it. 'We have to start on Monday!' she said.

Claire nodded and seemed to accept what Mandy told her. Slowly she went up the steps into her house.

Monday teatime arrived at last. Simon had arranged to bring Michelle straight to Rosa's Refuge. They arrived just as daylight began to fade.

Mandy was there early. 'Let's choose Spike and Speedy for the first day,' she said to James. 'They're nice and strong and healthy.'

James held Speedy, ready for Michelle to arrive, and Mandy herself held Spike. Claire was with them, wrapped in a blue anorak and scarf, ready and willing to help.

Michelle strode up and put her bag on the lawn. 'I've brought the transmitters,' she said. 'Are these the brave explorers who'll help us carry out our experiment?'

Spike blinked and snuffled. Mandy nodded. 'This is Spike.' She watched carefully as Michelle took out a thumbnail-sized metal tag with a tiny aerial attached to it.

'Great!' Michelle inspected him. 'He even has a little bald patch to which the transmitter could be attached!' She set to work, punching a tiny hole in the skin at the base of his ear to keep the tag in place.

Soon Spike was fixed up with the new tracking device. He sat quietly in Mandy's hand, snorting at the fresh air smells.

'He looks funny!' Claire giggled.

'He can hardly wait!' Simon laughed.

Michelle worked quickly to attach a second luminous tag and aerial to Speedy. Soon both hedgehogs were ready.

'Right,' Michelle said. She checked the two signals on her receiver. Spike's was a low and slow bleep, while Speedy's was high and fast. 'That's

fine. Are you ready?' she asked Mandy.

Mandy took a deep breath. 'Ready!' she said.

'We'll follow Spike first, OK?' Michelle asked.

Mandy looked down at Spike. His tag glowed bright green in the gathering dark. His signal bleeped loudly on Michelle's receiver. 'Good luck!' she whispered to him. And she set him down on the lawn.

'We've all got our fingers crossed for him,' Simon told her. 'Look, he's off!'

They listened and watched as Spike, with his little green light, snorted and darted for the nearest hedge.

'Come on!' Michelle said to Mandy. 'Just you and me – not too much fuss!'

But James said, 'Hang on!' and whispered something to Michelle.

Michelle nodded. 'OK, Claire, you come too!'

Claire shot forward to join Mandy and Michelle.

They followed the light at a distance of about thirty metres. It zigzagged from hedge to bush, then back to hedge. It circled the beech tree at the back of Rosa's Refuge, then it darted under a fence towards the woodland where Mandy had walked Blackie on Saturday.

'I can't see him!' Mandy whispered. She'd lost him in the long grass and undergrowth.

'No, but I can hear him loud and clear!' Michelle said. She followed where the low, slow bleeps came loudest. 'Look!'

They picked up the green light again, standing stock-still in the middle of a small clearing.

'Why has he stopped?' Claire wondered. 'What's wrong?'

She hadn't finished whispering before they saw the answer. Spike had picked up a scent and rolled into a tight ball. He'd smelt danger!

Out of the low laurel bushes opposite came the menacing shape of a fox! He must have heard Spike snorting among the leaves for slugs and come to investigate!

Mandy crouched in the long grass, afraid. Would Spike know what to do when danger came? She glanced across at Claire, then fixed her gaze on Spike's little green light and prayed.

The fox dipped his head towards Spike. He sniffed. He dipped his nose towards the hedgehog, but didn't touch the spikes. He put out one front paw, as if to tap the prickly ball.

At that second, Spike unrolled and prepared to sprint.

'Oh, don't!' Claire said. 'Roll up again, quick!'

The fox's jaw snapped within millimetres of Spike's back legs. Quick as a flash, Spike rolled up again, and when the fox made a second lunge, his nose met hedgehog spines, sharp and strong. He yelped, then howled, shook his head and sloped off. The clearing fell silent. Spike had won!

'A fox seldom gets the better of a hedgehog!' Michelle said, smiling. 'It's only badgers they really have to worry about! And that's only natural; badgers have to hunt and eat something, after all!'

Mandy nodded, relieved to see Spike unroll unharmed. He began to forage happily for food again. She felt pleased and proud for Spike as he set off on his first solo journey.

'I think we'll let him go off and roam on his own now,' Michelle said. 'We only have to worry about one more thing.' She paused as they watched Spike set off further afield, his green light glowing.

'What's that?' Mandy asked.

'Well, we've seen he can survive in the wild all right,' Michelle pointed out. 'But will he come back to his nest, or will he go off on his own and build new ones?'

Claire ran up to Michelle. 'You mean, will Spike come home?' she gasped. 'But won't he just come back in the morning, like Guy?'

Michelle shrugged. 'We'll have to wait and see. Come on. We'll try and pick up his signal again later if we have time! Now it's Speedy's turn!'

They turned back together through the dark woods.

Mandy and Claire looked over their shoulders every five seconds, but they'd lost sight of Spike's little green light.

'Oh!' Mandy said to herself. She felt exactly how Claire must have felt when she had to leave Scotland. 'It's the hardest thing in the world to say goodbye!'

Eight

On that first night of freedom Speedy lived up to his name. James held him as Michelle checked his radio transmitter. Claire took a second or two to say goodbye, then James set him carefully on the lawn.

Mandy watched as the fast little hedgehog paused for just one moment. Then he raced off at top speed, straight under the shed where Claire's father kept his lawnmower!

Michelle followed, with her radio receiver going bleep bleep bleep, fast and high. She shook her head. 'We'll never fish him out from under there!'

Mandy wondered why he'd made a beeline for the shed.

'Maybe there's an old nursery nest under there too!' Michelle said. 'One that Rosa built for her babies.'

Mandy got down on all fours to see if she could spot Speedy's green light. But she could only hear the snorts and snuffles of a very happy young hedgehog. 'Plenty of slugs and worms under there!' she reported.

Claire crouched down beside her. 'Do you want to get him out?' she asked.

Mandy nodded. 'We need to track him a bit further than this to check that he can manage,' she said.

So Claire went off and came back straight away with Guy's feeding dish. She tapped it loudly with a fork. 'Here, Guy! Here, Guy!' she called.

And sure enough, grizzled old Guy came snuffling out of the hedge bottom. Claire scooped some cat food out of a tin into his dish and set it on the grass near the shed. Guy sniffed hungrily, his pointed nose in the air. Then he headed for supper.

'He always comes when I call!' Claire said proudly. 'And I bet Speedy will too!'

They waited, all eyes on the dark shed. Soon Michelle's signal for Speedy grew stronger, and then the little green light appeared from deep under the base of the shed.

'He's coming!' Mandy whispered.

The green light edged into the open. They could just make out Speedy's tiny, domed shape. Slowly he came out and sniffed the air.

Guy raised his head from the dish and listened. He turned his blind head. Then he sidled around the dish, as if making space for a guest. Speedy watched and waited. Then, true to form, he came at racing-car speed to join Guy at supper.

Noses deep in the dish, the two new friends ate greedily.

'Well done!' Mandy whispered to Claire.

Claire beamed back at her. 'Guy will look after him!' she promised.

When the dish was empty, the old hedgehog sniffed the air. He listened and waited for Speedy, then set off steadily up the lawn towards the road, with the young hedgehog in tow. He listened again at the gate, sidling against Speedy to make him slow down too.

'Look, he's teaching him road safety!' James breathed.

Michelle smiled. 'He's just a wise old hedgehog, that's all,' she smiled.

They all watched fascinated as Guy and Speedy safely crossed the road. Michelle followed with her receiver, and she and Mandy stood by the fence opposite Rosa's Refuge watching Speedy's light criss-cross the field. 'Plenty of slugs in that long grass!' Michelle confirmed. 'And with Guy to give him good advice, I should think that Speedy's first night of freedom will be fine too!'

'Speedy can be Guy's eyes!' Mandy said. 'He can see for him. They'll look after each other!' She felt happy that the second baby was beginning to find his own way in the world. And she saw from Claire's proud smile that she was glad too.

'OK?' Michelle asked, packing away her radio gear. 'And ready for the dawn chorus? We have to be back here, ready and waiting, before daybreak!'

They all nodded. 'We'll be here!' they promised.

Mandy hardly slept at all that night. Even taking off her clothes and climbing into bed was hard to do. All her thoughts were with Spike and Speedy. When she did sleep, she dreamt of dark fields and woodlands where hedgehogs roam, and of moonless, misty nights.

She woke well before dawn. How were Spike and Speedy? Had they survived the night? Would they find their way back home? Mandy couldn't stop the questions in her head.

At first she refused breakfast, but Mrs Hope made her eat at least a scrap of toast and drink some tea. She made her wrap up well, hugged her, and wished her good luck.

Mandy liked the rough, warm feel of her mother's dressing-gown, and her dark red hair falling loose over her shoulders. 'Thanks,' she smiled.

'Is Simon coming here to collect you?' Mrs Hope looked out of the kitchen window at the foggy early morning sky.

Mandy nodded. 'Michelle and Simon are coming here first, then we're off to track Spike and Speedy.' She sighed. 'I only hope they come back!'

Mrs Hope looked at Mandy and smiled warmly. She put an arm around her shoulder. 'Whatever happens,' she said, 'you're doing your very best for those young hedgehogs. And that's the most anyone can ask!'

Soon Simon arrived, bleary eyed and pinched by the cold. Michelle sat in the van, wrapped in a huge padded jacket with a high, zipped collar. 'Hi!' she said to Mandy.

Being a wildlife radio presenter wasn't all fun, Mandy decided. They drove off in silence between shadowy hedges, lost in the mist. The hills were invisible and, except for the milk delivery van, the village was silent and empty.

They pulled up outside James's house before dawn had fully broken. Mandy went up to his door. James was waiting in the hallway and came out to greet her, looking nervous and worried. 'Do you think they'll come back?' he asked.

Mandy shrugged. 'I don't know. Anyway, come on!'

Claire too had watched Simon's van pull up in the lane. Wrapped in her blue anorak as usual, she was waiting for them on the lawn. The Rosa's Refuge sign creaked, hardly visible in the grey light. Michelle brought her receiver from the van and they all stood in a huddle on the cold, wet grass.

'What do we do now?' Claire asked.

'Wait. What else?' Simon said.

A crow rose from a branch high in the beech tree and flapped heavily over the lawn. The trees dripped in the heavy mist.

Michelle switched frequencies on her receiver. She concentrated hard, trying to catch any faint sound; either the slow, steady bleep of Spike's signal, or the rapid, high sound of Speedy's.

'Any sign?' Simon asked. He was beginning to look concerned. It was nearly daylight. Surely Spike and Speedy should have returned by now.

Michelle shook her head. 'No, they're not back yet. Sometimes the signal can get blocked by hedgebanks, or by a high wall.' She too looked serious.

Mandy stamped her feet on the cold ground. Her breath came out in damp clouds. Waiting was too much to bear. Quietly she walked the length of the lawn, up to Claire's front gate. Claire followed silently. They peered down the misty road. 'Where are you, Spike?' Mandy breathed. 'Where are you, Speedy?'

She stared and stared, and there, almost in answer to her worried call, were two little round shapes! They were easy to mistake at first for stones or clumps of earth, but they were moving

steadily towards her in the middle of the road, side by side. One had the telltale radio tag and antenna. One was old and blind.

'It's Speedy!' Claire cried. 'And Guy! They're back! Oh, Mandy, they've come home!'

Michelle and James came running up the lawn. The receiver bleeped loudly. 'I've got him!' Michelle confirmed. Then she began to speak excitedly, though quietly, into a small black tape recorder. 'The first of the hedgehogs to return to Rosa's Refuge is Speedy. The time is seven forty-five a.m. Speedy was released at ten past eight last night. His return, with a blind hedgehog, Guy, marks success for the Welford rescue team!' She pressed a button and beamed at Mandy. 'Good news!' she said.

'Look!' Mandy watched as Speedy circled once round Guy, then trotted off. He headed off down the lawn straight for his own nest-box, paused once at the little tunnel entrance, sniffed and vanished. Mandy breathed a huge sigh of relief.

'And here, right on cue, comes hedgehog number two!' Simon called. He peered over the hedge at the back of the McKays' garden.

The mist lifted as day finally broke, and Michelle's receiver was picking up Spike's low signal loud and clear. Spike trundled across the flower-beds, heading for home.

Michelle spoke again into her recorder, her voice quiet and dramatic at the same time. 'Spike, the second hedgehog, is arriving home at seven forty-nine a.m. He's in good shape and heading for his nest-box. There seems little doubt that both hedgehogs are fit and well, and easily able to survive in the wild!' She pressed the stop button. Spike was already inside his dry, warm box, even now fast asleep.

'Brilliant!' Mandy breathed. James grinned broadly. Claire ran and checked to see that Guy was safely home, then she joined them.

'Speedy came back!' she said, jumping up and down. She let out little clouds of steamy breath into the cold air. 'Guy brought him home!' She danced for joy.

'Tonight it's Tiggy and Scout's turn!' Mandy said.

'Don't worry, I don't need a reminder!' Michelle laughed. 'I'll be here!' She zipped up her shoulder bag. 'With two new transmitters and two new signals!' She turned cheerfully to Simon. 'This is great,' she said. 'Just what the listeners of *Wildlife Ways* want to hear!'

They all said goodbye, leaving Mandy, James and Claire to be rounded up and herded inside by Mrs McKay.

'Come into the warm!' she cried in her rolling voice. She was ready with hot chocolate and toasted teacakes, the kitchen cosy and clean. 'Now you three warm your feet and have plenty to eat,' she said. 'And then it'll be time for me to drive you into school!' She smiled; 'You've not forgotten about school, I take it!'

'No, but I wish *you* had!' James grumbled.

They all laughed.

'We want to have a celebration for Spike and Speedy!' Claire said. 'Don't we, Mandy?'

Mandy smiled. 'We are celebrating!' She held up her cup of hot chocolate. 'They're both safely back home!'

She paused and looked out of the window at Rosa's Refuge. James and Claire's bright, bold crossing warning showed up well in the daylight. The 'Rosa's Refuge' sign swung to and fro. 'But, really,' she said quietly and almost to herself, 'I suppose in a way we want them not to come home.' She sighed. 'We want them to be free!'

Nine

A misty dawn lifted into a perfect blue day. Mandy smelt the sharp autumn smells of leaves and earth as she cycled home from school. Tonight was Bonfire night. She saw groups of children collecting the last wood for their fires. Usually she would be one of them. But now all she could think of was hedgehogs.

She went home and quickly ate her tea, planning to meet Michelle at Rosa's Refuge. She planned to interview them for *Wildlife Ways*.

'Good luck to Tiggy and Scout!' Mr Hope called out from the surgery.

'Thanks!' Mandy looked in on him before she

set off. 'I'll probably stay on for Claire's bonfire after we've tracked Tiggy and Scout.'

'OK, take care!' he said.

As she cycled, she told herself everything would be fine again. Spike and Speedy had survived their first night, so why not Tiggy and Scout? Being hand reared obviously hadn't spoiled their chances of living wild again.

But Tiggy was so small and clumsy, she thought. Maybe she would need more protection than the others. She shook her head crossly, and told herself not to fuss. Simon and Michelle must think Tiggy was strong enough to cope. Tonight meant freedom for two more baby hedgehogs!

Michelle had already asked Mrs McKay if they could use her kitchen for the interview, so Mandy went into the lovely warm house to join James and Claire.

'Don't let the recorder put you off,' Michelle told Mandy. 'Just talk normally to me about how you rescued Rosa and then decided to set up a refuge, OK?' She held the slim machine in Mandy's direction and pressed some buttons.

Mandy swallowed hard. 'Well, I was very lucky because my mother and father are both vets at Animal Ark,' she began. 'So I knew we would be able to mend Rosa's broken leg. But I was very worried about her babies!' The story flowed as she recalled every moment of that dramatic time.

Michelle listened intently to Mandy and only rarely interrupted. Her silver earrings swung as she nodded her head. She smiled Mandy through each stage of the story.

'And once you'd established a feeding pattern for these young hedgehogs, were you ever tempted to make pets of them?' she asked.

'Oh, yes!' Mandy glanced at Claire and confessed. 'We would love to have kept them! They're beautiful animals, and people think they make sweet pets. You can feed them, and they'll come when you call,' she said.

'But?'

'But they belong in the wild!' Mandy said firmly. 'They have their own nests, and they like to wander. You mustn't try to keep them in a cage.'

She saw Claire nodding her head furiously, agreeing with every word!

'What happens if you do?' Michelle asked, putting the recorder closer to Mandy as her voice dropped.

'They fight to get out. And they usually die young!'

'Yes, so that's the idea behind Rosa's Refuge,' Michelle agreed. 'To get this whole family of hedgehogs back into the wild.' She turned the machine and spoke into it. 'Mandy Hope's hedgehog refuge is turning itself into a model experiment of its kind. As we heard, last night two of the young hedgehogs were set free, and both survived. Tonight it's the turn of the other two babies, part-reared in captivity, but now about to be released!'

Michelle pressed the stop button. 'Well done, that's great!' she said. 'You didn't sound at all nervous!'

'That's because I'm more worried about Tiggy and Scout!' Mandy confessed. She got up, anxious to start.

'OK, I'm with you!' Michelle said, grabbing her case of equipment. 'Let's go!'

Out in Rosa's Refuge with Simon, Claire and James, Mandy and Michelle made the hedgehogs ready. 'We need to set them off well before the bonfires get started,' Michelle said. 'Then they can be well away into the woods and fields, out of harm's way. We'll track them for the first hour or so, as before. After that, it's up to them. We'll be back in the morning, ready to check them in. OK?'

They all nodded.

Mandy was especially nervous as she took Tiggy, whose tag was now glowing green in the dusk. 'Ready?' she checked.

Michelle turned up the volume on her receiver. Tiggy's signal was a rapid double bleep, followed by a pause and then repeated. 'Ready!' she said.

Mandy lowered Tiggy to Claire's level so she could say goodbye. Then she put her on to the grass. The little hedgehog picked up her front feet one at a time, as if the wet, cold ground surprised her. But soon her nose went down to the earth and she snuffled off happily.

Safe journey! Mandy thought. The little green light headed across the garden towards the neighbour's beyond. Michelle went ahead with her radio. This time, James joined Mandy and Claire and they all followed.

Through a couple of gardens, grunting and snacking, Tiggy made her way. They began to breathe more easily. Perhaps she would be all right!

When she reached open fields, they could all

stand back and take a long-distance view of her.
The green light zigzagged smoothly and the
bleep-bleep-pause-bleep signal was strong. Then
the light rose mysteriously thirty centimetres or
so into the air, bobbed and vanished!

'It's OK, I've still got the signal!' Michelle said.

'Come on!' Mandy yelled, racing ahead.

They ran across the field. Underfoot the
ground grew wetter. Mandy's wellingtons sank
into soggy earth. 'There's a water trough!' She
pointed out the shape of an old enamelled bath,
now half sunk into the ground and in use as a
cattle trough in one corner of the field. 'Tiggy
must have fallen in there!' she shouted.

'She'll drown!' Claire cried.

Michelle held her hand. 'Don't worry;
hedgehogs can swim!' she said.

James got out his torch and shone it on to the
water. And there was Tiggy's little head, nose
above the surface and green light glowing, doggy-
paddling gamely round the water trough!

'She can't get out!' Claire gasped.

Bleep-bleep-pause-bleep! went Tiggy's signal.
She squeaked helplessly.

'Much more of that and she will go under!'
Michelle said. So Mandy quickly put on her glove

and guided the little swimmer towards one smooth, sheer side of the trough. There she could put her hand underneath Tiggy's belly and lift her safely out.

'She's exhausted!' Mandy said. 'Didn't I say you were accident-prone?' she scolded. 'Now, no more midnight swims!' She put Tiggy down and watched her waggle the water drops off her body.

Michelle and James laughed. Even Claire smiled. Soon Tiggy was off again, striking out towards a ditch and disappearing into the thick tangle of nettles and brambles. Her light vanished, but her signal continued strong and

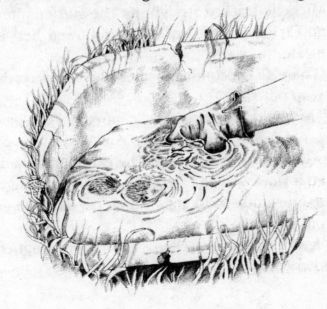

clear. They breathed another sigh of relief.

'Now for Scout?' Michelle suggested.

Mandy crossed her fingers for Tiggy and nodded. 'Now for Scout!' She felt easier about him somehow. Big and bold, he was the explorer.

Still she felt a pang as they went back to Rosa's Refuge and checked Scout's signal. His was a long, uninterrupted sound. He looked as funny as the rest with his little aerial attached to the glowing tag behind his ear, and Mandy, James and Claire wished him luck too as they set him free. Scout looked up at them, his head on one side. Then he was off!

Michelle tracked straight up the garden after him. Claire, James and Mandy followed her to the gate.

'There's a car coming!' James whispered, ready to leap out.

They held their breaths. Scout edged out into the road. He ignored the dip and sway of headlights down the road. The car approached, then it slowed. The "Hedgehogs Crossing" sign shone brightly in its lights. The car stopped as Scout scuttled on.

'It works!' James yelled. The others laughed and cheered.

From inside his car, the driver nodded and gave them a thumbs-up signal. Then he drove cautiously on.

'Come on, Mandy!' Michelle said. She crossed the road, hot on Scout's trail. 'He's really getting a move on. I think he's found a run!'

Mandy followed, through a field into a small group of oak trees. Scout's light was still in view, then it was gone, then back in sight! The long bleep came through strongly. All was well!

The oak wood was full of dark shadows and strange noises. Mandy wasn't surprised when Scout's light finally vanished for good behind some sturdy tree-trunk or thick undergrowth. Old trunks of knotted wood twisted into strange, almost living shapes in the dark, and bare branches stretched like fingers into the sky. The signal grew fainter and disappeared.

'Where's he gone?' Mandy whispered.

Michelle pushed buttons on her receiver, but she couldn't bring the signal back. 'Probably behind a hedgebank. It muffles the sound, remember?'

They searched on. They climbed over fallen tree-trunks and squelched through streams. But there was no sign of Scout.

'He really has gone exploring!' Michelle said at last. 'But just think of Spike last night, off on his travels. And he turned up safe and sound!'

Mandy nodded. 'OK, let's go back.' She sighed. 'There's no point in going on looking. Scout could be well out of range by now anyway!'

With a heavy heart she trudged back to Rosa's Refuge.

That night Claire had her bonfire surrounded by her new friends. Mandy stood beside her as Dr McKay lit a long torch of twisted newspaper and held it against some of the dry kindling at the base of the pile. Sparks carried on the wind and took light. Flames began to lick at the wood. The fire crackled and darted into the depths of the bonfire. Soon there was a fine blaze.

Mandy breathed in the smell of woodsmoke. Now the flames shot high, carrying sparks which danced in red swirls into the dark sky. 'It's a good bonfire!' Mandy said to Claire. 'And look over there!'

She pointed along the horizon above Welford, over to High Cross Farm and the Beacon. All along the way, other fires glowed; little patches of red light on the dark hillside. It made her feel

connected to those far-off gardens and the
children there.

Mrs Hope came and joined them as Claire's
fire began to settle and fade. She brought a
special Yorkshire treat of parkin for the McKays;
a cake baked by Gran, made of oats, treacle and
ginger. They stood around the fire, faces aglow,
munching the cake from gloved hands.

'How did it go tonight?' Mrs Hope asked
Mandy. She warmed her hands at the fire.

'Fine!' Mandy did her best to sound confident.
Her mother laughed at the story of Tiggy's un-
expected soaking. 'I'll be glad when tonight's over
though!' Mandy admitted. 'I just want to see Scout
and Tiggy safely back after their first night out!'

Mandy and Michelle arrived at Rosa's Refuge
first, before dawn on the Wednesday morning.
The smell of smoke lingered, and the sad ashes
of the previous night's bonfire. James and Claire
must both have slept in after the excitement of
the evening before.

'Shall I wake them?' Mandy asked Michelle.

'No, let them sleep in this morning. They
deserve it!' Michelle said. 'And we have to get a
move on.'

Michelle quickly tuned in her receiver for Tiggy's return and they wandered down the road in the direction of the field with the water trough. It was a grey, flat light. Nothing stirred. 'Seven-thirty a.m., Wednesday the sixth of November,' Michelle said into her recorder. 'And still no sign of either of the hedgehogs released last night.'

Mandy scanned the field. All her worry for Tiggy came flooding back. The minutes ticked by.

But then Michelle began to pick up a faint signal. 'Listen!' they said together. Soon the sound grew louder. They rushed forward in its direction through the wet grass.

'She's coming home!' Mandy said to herself. 'Even Tiggy!'

But there was another surprise in store. 'This signal is still very faint,' Michelle pointed out. 'And it fades every now and then, as if the aerial isn't working properly!'

They listened hard and at last heard the telltale snortings of a hedgehog stopping off for breakfast. 'Over here!' Mandy called.

She lifted the spiky branches of a blackberry bush. Beneath it, Tiggy foraged noisily. But since last night she'd managed to have yet another curious accident!

'What's that round her middle!' Michelle gasped. 'It looks as if she's wearing a belt!'

Mandy bent and picked Tiggy up. 'It's a plastic collar from a pack of drink cans!' she announced. They examined Tiggy carefully. 'No damage done! She must have nosed her way into some rubbish and crawled inside the ring without seeing it! Now she's stuck!'

'And she's bent her aerial,' Michelle said. 'No wonder we couldn't pick up her signal very clearly!'

In spite of themselves, they smiled at the comical sight. 'That piglet's a walking disaster!' Mandy admitted.

Michelle had to use a small penknife from her pocket to cut through the plastic ring and release Tiggy.

'Shall I put her down again?' Mandy asked.

Michelle straightened the aerial then nodded. She switched on her recorder. 'Seven forty-five a.m., and the smallest hedgehog has returned!' she said. 'Tiggy came home with an interesting fashion item in the shape of a plastic belt, but otherwise unharmed! We're watching now as she wanders along the run back to Rosa's Refuge. Success number three for the young team, though the night has certainly been an eventful one!'

Mandy shook her head and smiled as Tiggy finally crept through the hedge into Claire's garden.

'Three out of four!' Michelle congratulated her. 'That's not bad!'

But Mandy wanted four out of four. 'Let's go back and track Scout from where we last saw him!' she said eagerly. Her confidence was high; Scout was always the one who could look after himself.

So they retraced their steps across the road into the small oak copse. They stood where they'd picked up Scout's last signal. Michelle turned up the volume on the receiver; they met dead silence.

'He probably went much further than any of the others,' Mandy said. 'He likes to explore. He's a wanderer!'

'We could be in for a long wait,' Michelle agreed. She went forward a few paces, testing the undergrowth with her boot. 'Was it somewhere here that we lost the green light?'

Mandy thought she recognised a fallen tree-trunk and the huge, twisted bole of a tree. 'Just to the left there, I think,' she agreed.

'Ah!' Michelle paused.

'What is it?' Mandy tried not to panic. But Michelle sounded suddenly serious.

'Badger!' Michelle said. 'Here's its sett!' She pointed out a hidden tunnel, neatly dug, fairly large, surrounded by footprints and scuffed earth. She looked up at Mandy. 'This could explain things,' she warned.

Mandy shook her head. 'A badger wouldn't get Scout!' she protested. 'He'd roll up into a ball. He'd wait until the danger passed!'

Michelle frowned. 'Badgers have very strong front claws,' she explained. 'They can prise open a hedgehog, especially a young one.'

Mandy pushed at the bushes and ferns around the entrance to the sett. 'No,' she said. 'Scout would be able to get away!'

But Michelle had walked a few metres off, beyond the enormous oak. She stopped searching and stood up. In one hand she held a broken aerial and a small metal tag. 'Mandy!' she said gently.

Mandy felt her whole body go empty and limp. She stared at Scout's radio tag.

'There are signs of a big struggle,' Michelle said. 'The leaves are disturbed. Something pretty fierce has been going on here!'

Mandy forced herself to put one foot in front of the other to join Michelle. She gazed down at the ground and saw deep claw marks and a patch of blood on the leaves.

As Michelle put one arm around her shoulder, Mandy broke down in bitter tears!

Ten

Simon took Mandy home to Animal Ark. Mrs Hope listened to the news and nodded. 'We'll manage,' she said quietly. She took Mandy inside.

'Cry if you want to,' she told her. 'Here's a big box of tissues, so just go ahead!' She spoke gently, with one arm round Mandy's shoulder.

Mandy couldn't put anything into words. She just wished Scout was still alive. In her memory, she saw him clear as anything nosing out on to the lawn ahead of the rest to find that first dish of food. He was the bravest of Rosa's babies. Scout the explorer. Scout the fearless one.

'I understand,' Mrs Hope said. 'When you deal

with animals it's often sad. You know that yourself, Mandy. Pets get sick and die, don't they? We never want it to happen.'

Mandy nodded through her tears. 'I remember when James's cat, Benji, died.'

'And when animals live in the wild it's dangerous. They don't all survive. They have enemies; there are all sorts of accidents that can happen!'

Gradually Mandy stopped crying. 'I do know!' she agreed.

'And I know how you're feeling,' Mrs Hope said. 'Nothing I say will actually help you stop missing little Scout. Only time will do that.' She held Mandy's head against her shoulder. 'So what do you want to do? Do you feel up to going into school?'

Mandy sniffed and sat upright. She remembered James in school, quiet and pale on the day Benji died. 'Yes, I want to go in,' she said.

Mrs Hope looked at her and nodded. 'Good. I'll sort out a lift for you. We're a bit late for you to go in by bike.' She gave Mandy one last hug. '*Wildlife Ways* is on tonight, isn't it?'

'Yes. Michelle's spending the day editing the

tape,' Mandy told her. 'She has to get it ready for the broadcast.'

'That's terrific!' her mother said, smiling at her. 'I'm so proud of you, Mandy Hope!'

Before the programme came on the air, Mandy and the Operation Hedgehog team had one final task to complete. They had one more hedgehog to set free. At dusk that evening it was Rosa's turn!

Simon lifted her out of her nest-box. He asked Mandy to shine a torch on to the broken leg while he clipped away at the plaster bandage. Everyone stood around watching. Soon the leg was free. Simon felt it gently with his fingertips, then handed Rosa to Mandy. 'Feel it. It seems to be OK,' he said.

Mandy felt the injured leg. She had Rosa nestling in the gloved palm of her left hand and felt up and down the thin little leg with her right. No swellings, no bumps in the bone. 'As good as new!' she said. Rosa blinked happily and sniffed at the leather glove.

'I think so too!' Simon said.

Mandy took a deep breath. 'So, we're ready!' She put Rosa down on the lawn of Rosa's Refuge.

As she stepped back, she felt Claire come up and quietly take her hand.

Rosa settled on to the wet grass. Her nose twitched. She made a short run up the lawn, stopped, shunted sideways, then made a few circular runs for practice.

'No problem with the leg!' James laughed.

They all followed as Rosa trotted happily to the gate, smelling her way towards old, familiar runs. She scuttled through the gate and ambled down the roadside, past the 'Hedgehogs Crossing' sign towards James's garden gate. Then she made a sharp left turn up his path.

'Not again!' Mandy cried. Rosa was making straight for James's hallway.

'This is where we started!' James laughed. 'It's OK; Blackie's safe in the back of the house,' he promised.

They watched in disbelief as Rosa sniffed her way up the front step.

'Oh, no, your dad!' Mandy cried again. Mr Hunter had opened the front door to see what all the noise was about. Blackie scrabbled furiously against the kitchen door.

'Watch out, Dad!' James yelled.

Mr Hunter stood, legs wide apart, in his

stockinged feet. They all groaned as Rosa nipped in between his legs, straight into the hall!

'Don't move!' Mandy warned.

Mr Hunter looked aghast.

Rosa sniffed the doormat and zigzagged between his legs. 'Oh, look, she's coming back!' Mandy cried in relief this time, as Rosa half leapt, half rolled back down the step on to the path.

Thank heavens! They all sighed. Mr Hunter stood there, dumbfounded, shaking his head.

Two cars came down the lane, headlights catching the hedges and walls, as Rosa muddled along happily between flower-beds and garden seats in James's garden. Both cars slowed down when they saw the 'Hedgehogs Crossing' sign, and both drove slowly on down the road.

Rosa took not a bit of notice. She didn't venture back on to the road, but chose a path along the grass verge, under James and Claire's sign, back towards Rosa's Refuge. Mandy and her group tramped up the Hunters' path, out on to the road, and found her again. She was nosing her way into a feeding station to find her evening meal.

They waited while she munched and snorted.

'Look over there!' Claire pointed to a strange light glowing under their shed. 'I think it's Tiggy!'

'It is!' Mandy said. She recognised the wobbly walk.

Tiggy trotted forward as Rosa finished feeding. The two hedgehogs greeted each other with quiet, contented snuffles.

'I think she can get along without this now!' Simon said, as he went over and bent quickly to unclip the glowing tag and aerial. He smiled at Mandy.

Soon two more lights came floating out of the deepest shadows. Spike and Speedy had returned to greet their mother. When Simon had carefully removed their radio tags too, the family could get on with its reunion. Rosa circled her three children. She nosed each one in turn and circled them again. Then she retreated to the edge of the lawn. She watched as first Speedy, then Spike and Tiggy set off on their night's adventure.

Slow old Guy snorted loudly from the hedge to call Speedy, and they set off across the road as usual. Tiggy wobbled from lawn to path, then vanished into another hedge. A snort or two told them she was happily eating slugs for supper! Spike, minding his own business, cut behind the shed and headed for a new dark corner to explore. Soon all three were gone.

Mandy sighed. She watched Rosa turn and begin to root around under a tree. She spiked dead leaves on to her spines by rummaging deep into a raked pile of them.

'Nest building!' Simon told them excitedly.

'Where?' James asked. 'Does this mean she'll choose somewhere close by to hibernate?'

Simon nodded, then told them to watch closely. 'She's getting ready for a long winter's sleep!' he said, looking at his watch. 'And don't I wish it was me!'

Mandy smiled. If Rosa was getting ready to hibernate in Rosa's Refuge, it would be one more triumph for them! And soon Rosa, under her collection of dead leaves and grass, trotted back out on to the lawn.

'She looks like a moving compost heap!' James whispered.

'She's heading for her own nest-box!' Claire said. 'I think she's going to spend the winter in your box, James!'

Rosa busily snorted her way towards the box under the beech tree, carrying her winter bedding with her. She disappeared straight down the tunnel and didn't come out. They waited, but there was no sign of her; only the quiet creaking of the 'Rosa's Refuge' sign as it swung in the cold night wind.

Rosa's babies had gone foraging into the night – to eat, to build nests, to hibernate. Rosa herself had chosen lodgings closer to home. At last, Mandy, James, Claire and Simon could go in out of the cold.

They went into Claire's kitchen, where the radio was already turned on. Dr McKay had tuned it into the right station. 'Any time now,' he announced. 'Are you sure you're all ready for instant stardom?'

Mandy gave an embarrassed grin and went to sit in a far corner. She was trying to keep an eye on the comings and goings out in Rosa's Refuge. But the kitchen light against the dark sky turned the window into a mirror. She saw only her own reflection; blonde hair damp from the mist, her eyes dark and wide. She gave up and turned to face James and Claire. The music played for the start of *Wildlife Ways*.

Michelle's voice introduced itself. They sat and grinned at one another. 'We know her!' Claire said proudly. 'She's our friend and she's on the radio!'

Mandy agreed. How strange it was to hear someone you knew well.

'Shh!' Mrs McKay said. But really she looked as excited as the rest.

They heard Michelle describe the aims of Rosa's Refuge. And then there was Mandy's own voice, sounding to her like someone else entirely! 'That's not me!' she cried. She felt herself blush bright red.

'It is! Shh!' they all said.

'This week saw the greatest triumph for the Welford team!' Michelle went on. 'On Monday and Tuesday of this week, they managed to rehabilitate the hedgehogs back into the wild!'

They sat and listened to the story of Spike and Speedy's release and of their safe return. They listened to the account of the second night; Tiggy and Scout's journey to freedom. Michelle described how little Tiggy survived. 'Sadly, Scout was not so lucky,' she said. 'When he failed to return to Rosa's Refuge this morning, Mandy and I set out to search the area where we'd last seen him. We found clear signs of a fatal struggle with a badger.'

Tears were in all their eyes as they listened.

But Michelle went on to round off her report.

'Scout's death in no way lessens the success of the project,' she said firmly. 'Rosa's Refuge is a brilliant plan to help wildlife. It has been put into operation by a group of dedicated animal lovers. We think it is one of the best schemes for rescuing and rehabilitating hedgehogs that we have ever come across!'

She paused before signing off. 'Here on *Wildlife Ways* we wish Rosa's Refuge well. Long may it continue to help injured and underweight hedgehogs recover their strength and their ability to survive in the wild!'

Mandy looked proudly at her friends. Her eyes shone with happiness. 'Well?' she asked Claire.

Claire thought long and hard. 'Guy's still here. And Rosa's here!' she said. 'And any other hedgehogs who need a home can come into my garden and be looked after by me for as long as they like!'

Mandy looked towards Dr and Mrs McKay.

'Of course they can!' they both agreed. 'Rosa's Refuge is open for business!'

Finally Mandy looked at James in perfect contentment. 'Then long may it continue!' she said.

LUCY DANIELS

Badger
— *in the* —
Basement

Illustrations by Shelagh McNicholas

Hodder
Children's
Books

a division of Hodder Headline plc

Badger in the Basement

Text Copyright © Ben M. Baglio 1994
Illustrations Copyright © Shelagh McNicholas 1994
Created by Ben M. Baglio, London W6 0HE

First published as a single volume in Great Britain in 1994
by Hodder Children's Books

To Bette Paul

One

Mandy Hope sat watching her pet rabbits hopping across the lawn.

'Come on, come to me,' she called. 'Over here – come on!'

The two rabbits hopped towards her, stopping now and then to nibble the short, fine turf. They moved slowly towards her and Mandy made encouraging clicking noises at them. She smiled at them too, though her mother told her they couldn't recognise her smile. But Mandy always smiled at her rabbits just because they were her very own rabbits.

In a household where dozens of animals came

every day, Mandy took great pride in her own pets. Her adoptive parents were both vets; her home was Animal Ark, a surgery and hospital for sick and injured animals.

Mandy loved all of them, but it was good to have a couple of perfectly healthy creatures to herself. Still smiling, she put out a hand to lead them towards her, and clicked her tongue gently. For a moment they stopped and listened, quite still and alert, then slowly lolloped across the grass to her. It was so quiet in the garden that Mandy could almost hear their back paws thump the turf.

But just as they approached her hand, a louder thump sounded from the house. Startled, the rabbits scattered and Mandy heard her mother's voice cut across the garden.

'Mandy – have you got any homework?'

'Oh, Mum, you've disturbed the rabbits,' Mandy answered.

'Oh, I'm sorry, love. I wanted to catch you before you went down to your rabbits. Remember what Dad says – homework first, animals second! Pop them back in the run, now, please.'

That was easier said than done! The rabbits had scattered into the flower-beds so Mandy had a delightfully hectic race around the garden before they were safely gathered in.

'Here I am, Mum!' she called on her way through the kitchen.

'Oh, Mandy, just look at your shirt!'

Mandy looked down. She was wearing her favourite old denim shirt, rather dirty now after the rabbits had scrabbled all down it.

'Sorry, Mum. You did ask me to put the rabbits back in the run so I just picked them up from the flower-beds.' She looked sunnily up at her mother, knowing she'd be forgiven.

She was right. 'Oh well, if you want to wear that shirt tomorrow you'll have to wash it yourself; I'm off to yoga at the village hall right now.'

Mandy grinned. 'No, that's all right, I'll wear something else.' Mandy never did care what she wore, so long as she could discard her school clothes as soon as she arrived home. She watched her mother prepare for class.

Emily Hope was not much taller than her daughter, and, wearing black leggings and sweat-shirt, didn't look so very much older. Pulling her red curls up on top of her head, she leaned across and kissed her daughter.

' 'Bye, love. Dad's in surgery. I'll be back about eight. OK?'

'OK.' Mandy was used to being left in charge of the house. Theirs was an independent kind of family; both parents were very busy people, called out at all hours, running the surgery six days a week, with only Simon, the veterinary nurse, and Jean Knox, the receptionist, to assist them. And herself, of course; Mandy was always eager to help with the animals. Now, she happily waved her mother on.

' 'Bye, then, Mum – see you!'

One of Mandy's jobs was to sweep out the kennels and the animal hospital. So, with Mum safely out of the way, Mandy decided that was what she was going to do next. The homework could wait!

An hour later, Mandy had swept up, pausing only to stroke and soothe a few furry, fevered brows, as she always did straight after school. She couldn't always feed the animals; some were post-operative and would be sick, others were on special diets, but she loved coming in to see them every day to hand out lots of TLC, as Mr Hope sometimes called her treatments.

'A shot of penicillin, four hugs, five pats and half a kilo of Mandy's special Tender Loving Care,' he prescribed for any animal sick enough to have to stay in Animal Ark for a few days.

She'd just finished what she liked to think of as her 'round' when she heard her name being called again.

'Mandy! Mandy!' That certainly was not her mother this time. Mandy knew who it would be: Jean Knox, the surgery receptionist, in need of help, as usual. Jean was a warm, sympathetic receptionist but terribly absent-minded.

I'll bet she's lost yet another pen, Mandy thought as she opened the sliding door into the reception area. 'Can I help you, Jean?' she asked.

'Oh, Mandy, your father's so very busy just now.' The receptionist lowered her voice. 'That Pekinese, you know,' she almost whispered.

Mandy smiled at Jean's delicacy. 'That Pekinese' was in the middle of a difficult pregnancy and, as she was Mrs Ponsonby's pride and joy, she was at Animal Ark almost daily.

'So how can I help?' she asked, looking round. reception was empty at that hour.

'Outside, love – the man in that blue van; you can't miss it, it's blocking the entrance. But he won't come in, I've asked him. Will you go and take the details? I'm right in the middle of doing the records.' Jean peered at the computer screen

and began to pick at the keyboard as if it would
bite her.

Mandy was only too happy to postpone her
homework. She took a pad and pen and went out
to the carpark. She soon saw the old blue van
parked across the entrance, but there was no sign
of its owner. Puzzled, she went up and tapped on
the van door. A sharp, narrow-faced man opened
the window and leaned out.

'Yeah?' he asked, looking down at Mandy
suspiciously.

'I've been sent to get your details.'

He looked surprised, then disgruntled. 'I've
come to see the vet, not some kid.'

Mandy flushed. She was used to the clients
worrying about her handling their pets, but they
weren't usually so rude.

'Dad's busy just now,' she apologised. 'If you
give me all the details, it'll save time later.'

She flipped her pad open and held her pencil
ready, hoping she looked efficient, though it wasn't
easy, peering upwards at the driver.

'Your name, please?' she asked, brightly.

'Bonser.'

Mandy was puzzled. 'Is that you, or the dog?'
she asked.

'*Mr* Bonser,' he said. 'Old Dyke Farm. And the dog's just a dog; no fancy name. And no fancy hospital bill either, tell your dad. I'm not a rich man.'

Mandy leaned on the van door to write the notes on the pad. There were sprays of rust holes around the front wheel, she noticed, and the wing was badly dented. It was certainly a battered old vehicle. No wonder he was worried about the bill for his dog. Not that it would worry her dad: he'd treat the animal whether the man could afford it or not.

'Will you bring . . . er . . . your dog in now?' she asked.

'No, I won't,' he answered rudely. 'She won't let me move her. You'll have to get the vet out here.'

Mandy backed off and returned to Animal Ark. Luckily, Mr Hope was now free.

'That Pekinese, Pandora, will pay for our next holiday,' he greeted her. 'She's my best friend just now.'

'Well, there's a not-so-best-friend outside demanding you come and see his dog,' said Mandy.

Mr Hope finished scrubbing his hands. 'I'll be right out,' he said. 'And, Mandy . . .'

'Yes?'

'Remember, humans are animals too!'

Mandy often forgot that; she could handle just about any distressed animal, from sickly snakes to poorly parrots, but she was not always so understanding with their owners.

'People are sometimes rude when they're nervous,' Dad explained as they walked together to the carpark. 'Stress, you know.'

Mandy sighed. 'Well, I suppose he could just be worried,' she admitted. 'Even so, he *was* rude.'

Dad stopped and turned to face her, his dark eyes stern. 'I hope you weren't rude back?'

Mandy tipped back her head, shook her thick, blonde hair and looked up at him. 'No, I think I was quite polite,' she said, honestly.

'I'm sure you were, my love.' He grinned at her. 'And seething! Thanks for coping with him – let's go and see what we can do.'

Mandy almost wished she hadn't gone to see. The injured dog lay in the back of the van, on an old plastic sack. No basket, no box, just the half-conscious animal on the hard floor. Standing by her father's side, Mandy was tall enough to see the muddy, blood-stained creature, with a foxy, pointed face and shining, terrified eyes.

'Let's see, now, beauty . . .' Adam Hope leaned in and gently felt all over the creature, which snarled and snapped at him.

'Steady, now,' he murmured.

But the dog wasn't at all steady, and Mandy joined in with her father, making soothing sounds, calming it down.

'Fetch a blanket, Mandy, she's shivering with shock.' He shot an accusing glance at the owner, who didn't even notice. Mr Bonser stood back gloomily, whistling through his teeth, looking as sharp and foxy as his terrier.

When Mandy came back she noticed the cold silence between the two men. Her father must have had a taste of Mr Bonser's bad temper!

Expertly, Mr Hope wrapped the blanket like a sort of sling round the dog and gently lifted her out of the car. The little dog lifted her lip in a pathetic attempt to snarl.

'Come across to the surgery,' he said to Mr Bonser.

'I'm in a hurry,' he said. 'You just give me an estimate; I'll decide whether it's worth it.'

Mandy was horrified. The man spoke as if he'd brought his old van in to be mended, not a real live dog. She held her breath, waiting for Mr

Hope's sharp reply. But he'd already disappeared into Animal Ark, expecting them both to follow.

Mr Bonser made no move. 'Tell your dad to ring me later.' He turned back to the van. 'And tell him if the treatment's too dear he'll just have to get rid of the dog. Don't forget, now!'

He made a sudden dart into the vehicle, turned on the ignition, pressed hard on the accelerator and swept out of the carpark.

Mandy leapt out of the way and watched him pull out into the lane without stopping. He could have caused an accident, she thought indignantly. And she thought of his dog; somebody had

certainly caused an accident to happen to her. And Mr Bonser wasn't even prepared to pay for treatment! Mandy flushed with indignation at the idea. How could he say such a thing? Well, one thing was certain: the little dog would get the best treatment at Animal Ark, whether Mr Bonser agreed or not.

Mandy made her way indoors. In reception she paused, part of her longing to follow Mr Hope into the surgery, part of her accepting that he wouldn't let her in just then; she'd just get in his way. She sighed and turned back into the house. The homework was still waiting.

Two

' . . . and she hasn't even got a name, you know,' Mandy said indignantly. 'The poor little animal!'

James said nothing. He was peering through the misted-up window, looking as miserable as the weather. It had been raining hard that morning so they'd taken the bus to school and now they were on their way home, packed in amongst the damp Walton shoppers.

'You're not listening,' Mandy accused him. 'You haven't heard a word I've said.'

'What?' James shook his head. 'Sorry,' he muttered. 'I was watching the rain.'

'That won't stop it,' said Mandy.

'No,' he agreed, dolefully. 'And I was looking forward to the first outing of the Welford Wildlife Watchers. We're going up to Piper's Wood with Walter Pickard, badger watching.'

'You're going to get wet, then,' said Mandy. The Welford Wildlife Watchers had just been formed and James was a very keen member. Mandy wished she could join, too, but most of her time was taken up with the sick animals at Animal Ark. 'Listen, I was telling you about this dog that was brought in yesterday evening . . .'

She repeated the whole story, and this time James listened.

'But your dad'll treat the dog even if that man won't pay,' James said. 'He always does.'

Mandy knew this only too well. She'd sat through many a discussion at the kitchen table, listening to her parents trying to balance feed figures and drugs bills against unpaid accounts and their own sympathy for suffering animals.

'I know Dad won't let a healthy dog die if there's any chance of saving her,' she said, standing up as the bus came into Welford.

James moved down the empty bus after her. 'And is there a chance of saving her?' he asked.

Now Mandy's blue eyes were serious. 'He'll save

her,' she assured him. She jumped off the bus at the Fox and Goose and waited for James to join her. 'But what's the point of saving the poor animal and sending it back to that Mr Bonser if he's not even interested in her?' she asked angrily.

'Well, it is his dog,' said James, reasonably.

'But some people aren't fit to keep a dog,' Mandy sniffed, quite upset at the thought of Mr Bonser taking the dog back. ' 'Bye!' she called to James and she turned and walked quickly up the lane to Animal Ark.

Her first call was to the modern extension built at the back of the old cottage. It always amused Mandy that both her home and her parents' business was called Animal Ark. But she loved the idea of living in an ark full of animals. Ignoring the entrance to the cottage, she went round the side into reception.

'Hi, Simon!' she called. 'How is she today?'

The surgery nurse looked up from the desk, where he appeared to be putting a camera away. 'Pandora Ponsonby, you mean?' he teased.

'No, you know, the little terrier.' Torn between wanting the dog to be cured and not wanting to send her back to the unsympathetic Mr Bonser,

Mandy was not in the mood for teasing.

Simon was quick to understand. 'Come and see,' he said. He led her down the corridor to the little room where the dog lay.

'She's still sleeping a lot,' he told her. 'We've pinned the leg and stitched her chest. So long as there's no further infection she should pull through. Trouble is, she's not in good condition. Looks half-starved to me.'

Mandy wasn't squeamish; she peered closely at the sleeping animal. She could always cope with sick or injured creatures, clean them, hold them, mop up all kinds of unspeakable messes, but she hated to see them in pain. It was one of the things that worried her when she thought of becoming a vet.

She bent over the sleeping terrier and swallowed hard. The wounds went right round the little dog's chest, deep and curved though neatly stitched and clean, now. 'What could have happened to her?' she asked Simon.

He shrugged. 'Looks as if she was attacked.'

'But who would do that to a little terrier?' Mandy asked, horrified.

'What, not who,' Simon explained. 'Some kind of fight, I should think.'

'With another dog?'

Simon shook his head. 'I'm not sure,' he said. 'These wounds don't look like dog bites somehow.'

'A cat, perhaps?'

'It would have to be some special sort of cat!' said Simon. 'And I don't think we have panthers round Welford!'

Mandy looked thoughtfully at the sleeping terrier. 'Wasn't there some sort of wild cat reported, hiding in the woods last winter? People found tracks and sheep were attacked. Do you remember?'

Simon nodded. 'I remember the newspaper reports,' he said. 'But I think it was all a hoax. The only wild cat round here is Walter Pickard's Tom – you should try giving him an injection!'

'Well, whatever it was, it's left some odd-looking marks,' Mandy observed.

'Yes, I've been taking a few photographs for the records.'

Mandy took another peek at the patient. 'Is she unconscious?' she asked Simon.

'Just sleeping,' Simon assured her. 'I gave her a jab to make her drowsy; she mustn't move that leg just yet and she's a bit of a chewer so it's best to keep her sleeping.'

As if to defy Simon, the terrier shifted in her sleep and whimpered. A wash had revealed patches of white amongst the sleek brown coat, and a patch of white over one eye.

'Another Patch,' murmured Mandy. Patch was the name of a kitten Mandy had rescued and given to the Spry twins.

'Now, Mandy,' Simon warned her. 'That's not her real name.'

'She hasn't got a real name,' said Mandy, sadly.

'Well, it's not up to us to give her one. Come on, now, let's leave her in peace.'

He was right, of course, Mandy thought, as she followed him out. It was one of Dad's rules for Animal Ark that animals must be called by the name their owners gave them.

But Patch hasn't got a name, Mandy argued to herself as she went up to her room to change out of her school clothes. *She's got an owner and a home and yet she hasn't got a name.* How could someone keep a dog and never give it a name? It was very odd, even for Mr Bonser.

But Mandy had no more time to ponder on the mystery. She had her rabbits to feed and several sick animals to visit before supper, *and* a stack of homework after.

She was just finishing her history when James rang.

'Mandy, have you still got *Secondary Mathematics*, Book Two?' he asked, anxiously. 'I've just been promoted to it and I've left mine at school.'

Mandy grinned into the phone; James was excellent at maths, already a whole book ahead of his year. Luckily, she'd not yet finished Book Two herself.

'Don't tell me!' Mandy reached for her school-bag. 'I'll get Simon to drop mine in on his way past. All right?'

'Great – thanks ... er ... how's the dog?' James asked eagerly, just as Mandy was about to replace the receiver.

'Patch?' she said brightly. 'Oh, she's all right; a bit weak and sleepy.'

'Thought you said she hadn't got a name?'

'She hasn't, that's just my private name for her.'

In the silence that followed, Mandy could almost hear James's thoughts. He knew that Mr Hope was usually quite strict about not giving animals names. She waited for him to remind her.

But James merely coughed a little and said, 'The badger watch was called off after all.'

'Why? Were the Welford badgers too busy to

watch Welford Wildlifers?' she joked.

'You're nearly right. The badgers have disappeared from their sett in Piper's Wood.'

Mandy felt a sudden spurt of interest. 'Where to?' she asked.

'Who knows? I just got a message to say the meeting was called off. So I'll get on with the maths instead. Thanks again for the book.'

'OK – 'bye!' Mandy put down the phone and sat back. She was thinking furiously, and not about history. Somewhere at the back of her mind an idea stirred. What was it Simon had said about Patch's wounds? 'A special sort of cat!' And now, down in Piper's Wood, the badgers had gone. Why? Frightened off, perhaps, by the same cat that had attacked Patch?

'Have we got any books about badgers?' Mandy asked her dad over supper.

'Since when have you been interested in badgers?' he asked.

'Since now,' she grinned back at him. 'So where are the books?'

Mr Hope's study was lined with books and those that didn't fit on the shelves were piled in heaps on the floor. Mrs Hope often offered to sort them out for him, but her husband knew she was joking;

he couldn't bear anyone to disturb them. Meanwhile, only he could find anything in there.

Together, he and Mandy went across the stone-slabbed hall into the oldest corner of the cottage. Mandy loved the study, with its slightly musty smell of books and paper. It was a long, low room, with a thick single beam running the length of the ceiling. The bookshelves ran right along three walls, even up to the deep-set windows at the end where Grandad's big old desk stood. The desk was so big that Mandy could have walked across it, and often had done, when she was younger.

Mr Hope was browsing through a pile of papers on the desk. 'Ah, yes, here we are . . . I knew I'd seen an article about the local badgers recently.' He handed her a rather boring-looking magazine, small and tightly printed.

Mandy flipped through the pages. 'There aren't any pictures,' she complained.

'I thought it was information you wanted, not pretty pictures.'

'A bit of both, Dad, please.'

Mr Hope turned to a low shelf where big books were stacked flat in a pile. He cocked his head and muttered to himself as he checked the titles.

'Mmm . . . here we are: *British Mammals of the*

Night. That's got some amazing photographs.'

Mandy took the huge book. 'Thanks, Dad,' she said. 'I'll be very careful with it.'

'You thinking of joining Welford Wildlifers then?' asked her father, curiously.

'Just doing a bit of research,' said Mandy.

Next day the rain had cleared so Mandy cycled to the Fox and Goose crossroads to wait for James.

'Hi, did you get the maths done?' she asked.

'Yeah – easy,' he puffed.

'Good, that means you're free this evening.'

James nodded. 'Got something for me to do at Animal Ark?'

'I've got something for you to do in Piper's Wood.'

He glanced quickly at her. 'Why Piper's Wood?'

'I want you to show me where the badgers live.'

'But I told you, they've gone.'

'I know, but I just want to see where they used to live. OK?' Mandy trod hard on her pedals and spurted ahead. 'See you later!' she called back.

'Sooner!' James yelled. 'Watch out, here I come!'

They arrived at the back entrance to the school in a dead heat, which made up for their late start. And as she worked her way through the busy school day, Mandy was haunted by the thought of Piper's Wood. She had no idea what she would find there, only a feeling that she had to go. The photograph in *British Mammals of the Night* had clearly shown a large male badger, digging a hole at the foot of a tree. Digging with two strong, black paws which ended in a set of strong, sharp claws.

Mandy recalled her conversation with Simon about Patch's injuries and shuddered. Any cat who could frighten a fully-grown badger would have to be a supercat!

Three

Mandy leaned on her bike's handlebars, sniffing deeply. After the previous day's rain, the beech woods gave off a pungent, musky smell.

'Mmm . . . !' she breathed. She loved the smell of the trees; it reminded her of damp autumn walks. She stirred the leaf-mould with her feet.

'Mandy – are you coming?' James had already hidden his bike in the bushes and was waiting for her.

Mandy shook off her daydream, turned and shoved her bike deep into the bushes too. Time for business – whatever that was! She wasn't sure exactly why she wanted to see the badger sett –

after all, it was empty. But there was just that niggling thought that there might be something important there.

James was leading the way, pushing through brambles and bracken with confidence. Mandy followed cautiously in his wake. It was all right for James; he often went rambling about in the undergrowth. But she preferred the bridle-paths. At least you knew where to put your feet there, she thought, stumbling over a hidden root and pitching forward.

'Ow!' she yelled. And she fell on to James's back.

'Hey! Go steady!' he cried.

'I can't go at all, unless you get a move on,' Mandy pointed out. 'Go on then!'

But James didn't move. 'Hang on, I'm just checking our position,' he said.

'We're lost, aren't we?' Mandy joked.

'No, not lost. Not really . . .' James began to move on, rather slowly. 'There should be a clearing somewhere here.' He peered through his glasses at the tangled bushes.

Mandy, a head taller, stretched up and surveyed the scene. Straight in front lay more brambles leading into thick woods; no sign of a clearing there. She stood on tiptoe and looked all round.

'The clearing's that way.' She pointed over to the right. 'Look, where the sun's coming through.'

James stretched upwards but he still couldn't see above the brambles. 'You'd better lead the way,' he admitted.

Mandy stepped out firmly now, ignoring the prickles and tangles. Pressing ahead, she soon reached the edge of the clearing.

'Here it is!' she called, triumphantly. She turned to wave to James, lost her balance and fell backwards down a grassy bank.

'Enjoy your trip?' James joked as he helped her up.

'You might have warned me,' protested Mandy.

James looked about him. 'You found the right place though. The badger sett is under those big trees.' He set off across the clearing.

Mandy brushed herself down and followed, muttering to herself. 'I might have sprained my ankle, or even . . .'

She stopped when she saw James. He was standing quite still, looking at the remains of a sandbank as if he'd seen something quite nasty in there. As she got close, Mandy could see that his face was white and grim, his eyes shiny behind his glasses. Mandy followed his glance but saw nothing more than heaps of sandy earth.

'Looks as though someone's been digging,' she said, puzzled.

James nodded, turned away from her, sniffed hard then took off his glasses and rubbed them on his jeans. After a moment he replaced the glasses and looked again at the mess.

'But why?' asked Mandy. 'What were they digging for?'

James took a deep, shaky breath. 'Badgers,' he answered, and sat down suddenly on a tree-stump.

Mandy gazed at the earthy bank with horror. She'd read enough of her father's book to realise that not everyone shared James's enthusiasm for badgers. Some people regarded them as pests. And she remembered that her mum had pointed out a letter from Sam Western in the local paper only a few weeks ago. He was complaining about people who wanted to protect badgers and foxes – 'vermin', he called them – and he claimed that they spread diseases amongst farm animals and should be rooted out.

'So where are the badgers now?' she asked James.

He shrugged. 'If they're lucky they've run away.'

'And if not?'

'Dead,' he said in a flat tone. 'Some people will hunt anything that moves.' He wiped a hand across his cheek.

Mandy was silent. She knew that some wild creatures were a nuisance to farmers, who had to protect their crops and animals. Vermin had to be put down; it was one of the hard facts of the countryside. But there were right and wrong ways of doing it. This looked like a rather nasty way to her.

'How do they kill them?'

He didn't look at her. 'They sometimes use gas, or send dogs to sniff them out . . .' He couldn't go on.

But Mandy knew what he meant. She'd read reports in the local paper about badger digging. A dog was sent down into a sett to face a badger. When the men above heard the barking, they knew just where to dig to get the badger out. Sometimes the badger would attack the dog and the men would let them fight it out. It had said in the book that a full-grown badger could injure, or even kill the kind of small dog used in this 'sport'.

A tremor of excitement went through her. Suddenly she knew what had drawn her to this place. What if Patch had been one of those dogs? And what if Mr Bonser had found her lost in the woods and was going to let her try again?

She turned to ask James, but one look at his face stopped her. He was gazing round hopelessly, scrubbing at his glasses now and then, as if to clear them. Mandy waited for a moment before speaking.

'Maybe all the badgers got away,' she said, hopefully.

But he wouldn't be comforted. 'No chance,' he said. And he went on scuffing his shoe in the soft earth, sniffing hard.

Mandy swallowed hard; she couldn't speak. She knew James was very upset too, but he wouldn't want her to fuss. She sat down beside him, quietly wiping her eyes with a grimy hand and watching his foot moving to and fro across the tracks in the soil.

'Hey, stop a minute!' She peered down at his feet. 'Look at this!'

James's foot stopped moving. 'What is it?' he asked.

'Look!' said Mandy again. 'These are tracks.'

'So?' James wasn't impressed.

'Well, maybe the people who came to dig out

the badgers drove up in a car.'

'I'm sure they did. They wouldn't come on their bikes, would they?' said James.

Mandy felt she wanted to shake him but remembered how upset he was and tried to be patient. 'Well, I'm going to follow the tracks,' she said, and set off, hoping he would follow.

She didn't get very far; once away from the loose earth, the tracks disappeared, though the undergrowth was flattened down where the car had driven through. Disappointed, Mandy followed the tracks back to the sett, where they were quite clearly imprinted in the sandy loam. She knelt down to examine them closely. They were wide and rather squashed. Well, whatever the vehicle was, it was bigger than a car. She put her face almost on to the soil. The prints were not as sharp as she'd expected in such soft earth. Rather blurred, as if the tyres weren't very good . . .

Mandy stood up with a surge of excitement.

'James, come over here, I think I've found something,' she called.

James sighed and dragged himself up. 'It's no use, Mandy,' he said. 'There's no sign of badgers here, now.'

'Well, there are plenty of signs of humans,' said Mandy. She stood and waited for James to come and see.

But James wasn't even listening to her. He was standing quite still, close to the sett, head down, one hand held up. 'Shh . . . !' he said.

'But . . .'

'*Listen*!' he whispered.

Mandy stood still and listened. She heard the wind gently sighing through the branches, sounding like a distant sea. Nothing else, except . . . yes, a small, miaowing sound. Alarmed, she looked over to James.

James stood for a moment, almost sniffing the air, then crept forward, steadily, silently, towards the remains of the sett. Once there he paused again, waited, and then bent to push aside the pile of loose earth with his hands. Then he knelt down and started scrabbling through the earth, like a dog after a bone. Before she could go to help, Mandy saw him gently lift something up out of the ground.

'What have you found?' she asked, moving over to join him.

'Shh . . . !' James said again. But he turned and showed her what he was holding. It was small and

helpless. It was a badger cub.

Mandy moved forward; she could see the little creature cradled in James's arms, shuddering now and then, and whimpering as if it was having a bad dream. Its coat was pale, hardly grey at all, the stripes barely visible on his head, and its nose was still rounded, not sharp. Its claws were already growing, though, and tangled in James's sweater.

'Oh, poor thing, left behind all on his own,' said Mandy, her voice full of anxiety.

'Lucky for him,' said James, grimly. 'He must have got buried by a fall of earth so they missed him.'

They both looked down at the little badger. Even as they watched, he raised his short snout and pushed it hard against James's sweater.

'He's hungry,' said James. 'That's how they feed, pushing down into the ground for worms and insects.'

'Well, maybe you should put him back then,' said Mandy.

James shook his head. 'He might be hurt,' he said. 'And anyway, I think he's too young to survive on his own.'

Mandy looked at the badger. She looked at James. 'So what are you going to do?' she asked, although she knew the answer.

It took them much longer than usual to get from Piper's Wood back to Animal Ark. James had wrapped the badger up in his sweater and tied it by the sleeves over his handlebars, like a little hammock. The cub was half-starved and exhausted, so he kept quite still in his woolly prison. Even so, James decided to walk, pushing his bike with one hand and balancing his burden with the other. Mandy rode slowly ahead, frowning to herself, thinking of the reception they'd get back home.

'*You'd* better take the badger to Animal Ark,' she told James. 'There's more chance of keeping him then.' Mandy was just as keen as he was to help the little badger, but she knew there would be problems.

James merely nodded and smiled. He would have agreed to anything just then, so long as the cub was safe.

He'd no idea of the trouble he was causing, Mandy thought. Wild animals were always difficult to keep at Animal Ark. They brought their own infections and even caught new ones from the tame animals. They had to be kept quite separately,

Mr Hope was always very firm about that, and that caused more work for everybody.

Mandy cycled slowly on to Animal Ark, partly to keep pace with James but mostly because she knew they were headed for trouble. She glanced back and saw James puffing after her, clutching the bicycle saddle with one hand, steadying the badger's hammock with the other. *Poor James*, she thought. *I hope we're not in for a disappointment.*

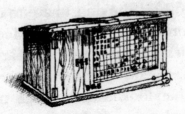

Four

'I'm sorry, but there it is,' Emily Hope spoke sadly. 'This is a veterinary practice, not a wildlife sanctuary.'

'But Dad's had wild creatures here before,' Mandy protested. 'Mr Bell brought that squirrel in after its mother was run over.'

'That's just the point, Mandy,' said her mother. 'Once that squirrel was treated, Ernie took it home; it wasn't at Animal Ark for long. But this little chap isn't even ill. He just needs a bit of food and shelter, and then what's going to happen to him?'

Mandy looked at James. He was holding the cub,

still swaddled in his sweater, and gazing ahead, blindly. Mandy could tell he was too upset to argue with her mother. She'd just have to try again.

'Mum, honestly, we'll do all the feeding. It'll be half-term next week and we'll be around all the time.'

Her mother looked at Mandy's pleading eyes and sighed. 'I know you'd take care of him,' she said, gently. 'And I'd love to give you the chance, but where will you put him? We simply can't risk putting a wild animal into the residential unit. One case of cross-infection and we'd lose our licence.' She put an arm round Mandy's shoulder and smiled sympathetically at James. 'I'll ring the wildlife sanctuary to see if they'll take him.'

At this, James woke up. 'But they're so overcrowded,' he protested. 'He doesn't want to go there.' And he clutched his bundle so hard that the badger squeaked.

Mrs Hope sighed. 'The sanctuary is busy just now, I know, but they do take good care of wild animals.'

Mandy looked at James's anxious face, then at her mother. 'Well, look, can we have a cage please, Mum?' she asked. 'Then at least we can make him comfortable for a while.'

Mrs Hope nodded. 'Of course,' she smiled. 'But make sure it's an old one; we may have to get rid of it later – and don't go into the surgery. There'll be a few old cages at the back of the garage.'

Mandy groaned; she knew when she was beaten. Mum was always reasonable, quite sympathetic – and very firm. She wouldn't give in. Sighing, Mandy led James across the yard.

Mr Hope was checking his emergency pack in the Land-rover. 'What have you got there?' he asked, seeing the bundle.

Mandy's heart sank as she watched James proudly presenting the little badger. Her dad looked very serious when they told him of their dilemma.

'Mum's right, you know,' he said. 'We can't risk infection – either for Pandora the peke or for this little chap.' He smiled and stroked the cub's snub nose gently.

'But he's got to have a home,' Mandy protested.

'First things first,' said her father. 'Let's see if we can find him a cage.' He looked under a shelf and came up with a rather battered travelling cage. 'Will this do?' he asked.

James looked doubtful, but even he realised that he couldn't keep the badger wrapped up in his sweater much longer. Mandy lined the cage with newspaper and filled it with straw. There was always plenty of both stored in the garage. James unrolled his sweater from the little cub and placed him gently down. The cub immediately began snuffling around and trying to nibble at the wire mesh.

'He needs food,' said James, looking worried.

Mr Hope reached into the Land-rover and took a packet from his box. 'This Vita-milk will keep him going for a while,' he said. 'We use it for bottle-feeding premature kittens and pups.' He peered closely into the cage and pushed a finger through the wire mesh. 'I think he's probably too old to suck . . . ow!' He cried and held out the finger. 'Yes, well, I asked for that, but at least it proves he's got his teeth! He'll manage a few pellets too. Mandy, you've got plenty of rabbit pellets – bring him a handful.'

They all stood round and watched as the badger lapped up the milk-mixture from a saucer and then snuffled through the straw after the pellets. When he'd finished he raised his little blue-and-white striped muzzle up to the bars of the cage, as if begging for more.

'What a little humbug!' murmured Mandy.

'What?' asked James.

'He doesn't belong to anyone, so let's call him Humbug,' said Mandy, smiling down into the cage.

But James still looked unhappy. 'It's not a name he needs, it's a home,' he said.

'What about your place?' suggested Mandy.

'My mum and dad won't allow wild animals in the house. They say that Blackie and the new kitten are quite enough for one house . . . and, anyway, there's nowhere for a badger to live at home,' he said. 'He needs a quiet, dark place for most of the day.'

Mr Hope nodded. 'Yes, of course he does, and a bigger cage with a separate sleeping area. Badgers are very particular about keeping their bedding clean.'

'We could make him a hutch,' said Mandy. 'Then he can go out on the lawn with my rabbits.'

'Not unless we want it digging over,' said her father. 'He may be a youngster but have you seen his claws?'

Mandy grinned. 'And then Grandad would be after him,' she said. 'Our lawn is his pride and joy. That's why he made me a new hutch . . .' She stopped, her eyes wide.

'So what did he do with the old one?' asked James.

'Put it in the basement back at Lilac Cottage.'

Mandy looked at James. He looked almost hopefully back at her. 'A basement's bound to be rather dark,' he said, thoughtfully.

'Come on!' commanded Mandy. 'I think a visit to my grandparents is in order!'

Mandy's grandfather was in his greenhouse, as usual.

'Hello, Mandy my love – and James. Come in – no, on second thoughts, there won't be room.' He came out to the driveway, shaking compost from his hands. 'Well, this is a nice surprise,' he smiled. 'Let's go into the kitchen and see if there's any tea.'

James looked frantically at Mandy. He couldn't bear to waste time having tea when his badger was still homeless. But he was too polite to say so.

Mandy understood. 'Well, actually, Grandad, we need your help first,' she said, and she told him all about finding the cub. 'So you see, we need that old rabbit hutch and a bit of space in your basement,' she finished.

Mr Hope looked thoughtful. 'Well, you can

certainly have the hutch,' he said. 'But as for letting
a badger into our basement, well, you know what
your gran is like!'

Mandy nodded; she knew her gran was devoted
to Smoky, the kitten Mandy had given her, and *he*
certainly wouldn't welcome a badger as a
companion.

Still, first things first, Dad had said. 'Well, may
we go and look for the hutch, Grandad?' she asked.
'We can talk to Gran about the basement later.'

She took James to the back of Lilac Cottage,
down a set of steep, stone steps and into a dark,
musty room below ground level. It had probably
been a cold-store for milk, butter and cheese long
ago, but now it housed the central heating boiler,
garden tools long past their best, drying-out bulbs
and rolls of spare carpet. It was warm and dry but
too dark to be of much use; 'Tom's junk heap,'
Gran called it.

Mandy pushed open the green wooden door
and peered round in the dusky light. 'Hang on a
minute, there's a light switch over the other side,'
she said.

'No – wait,' James spoke urgently. 'This is just
the right place for him, Mandy. It's dark and
peaceful and warm, and we could look after him

easily here. Do you think . . . ?'

'That Gran would let us use it?' Mandy sighed. 'Tell you what, James,' she said. 'Perhaps if we stay for tea we can persuade her.'

'Well, at least we can make him a comfy home,' said James. 'Where's that hutch?'

They soon found the hutch on a shelf by the boiler. It was quite clean and dry and Grandad came down and found old newspapers and wood shavings for the lining.

As they hunted for the shavings, Mandy explained to her grandfather that they wanted to make sure that the badger-diggers wouldn't come back to Piper's Wood.

'But how can you do that?' he asked.

'Well, there are tyre tracks all round the sett,' Mandy explained. 'They might prove who was there.'

Mr Hope nodded thoughtfully. 'You'll have to be quick off the mark,' he said. 'Tracks soon wash away if it rains. But don't you go hanging about the woods on your own, Mandy. Badger-diggers are not very pleasant folk.'

Mandy promised that she wouldn't do anything stupid. 'But you do see, don't, you, Grandad,' she said anxiously, 'why we've got to keep Humbug for a while?' Mandy and James waited for a reassuring reply.

But he merely suggested they all went upstairs to see whether Gran was home from her Women's Institute meeting at the village hall.

They found her in the kitchen, already getting tea. 'You'll stay and have some tea with us, won't you?' she beamed at them both. Mandy stared hard at James. This was their chance to persuade Gran to let them use the basement.

'Er . . . thank you, Mrs Hope,' he stammered. 'It's very kind of you.'

They hadn't realised how hungry they were. It was hours since school dinner and Mandy had been in such a hurry to get to Piper's Wood that they hadn't even stopped for a snack. Now they were able to do full justice to Gran's toasted tea-cakes and her gorgeous sticky parkin, all dense and dark and gingery.

Mrs Hope kept the inside of Lilac Cottage as beautifully clean and neat as Grandad did the outside. Which made the question of keeping a badger in the basement even more difficult. As she chatted on, Mandy could feel James's eyes on her; he was desperate to get away but even more desperate to find a home for Humbug.

'Well, thanks, Gran, that was lovely,' Mandy said, over-enthusiastically, as she stood to leave. When she didn't actually move to the door, her grandmother looked at her quizzically.

'Is there something you want, Mandy, dear?' she asked.

'What? Er, well . . .' For once, Mandy didn't know how to begin. She'd already told Gran about their trip to the woods and about finding the cub but hadn't mentioned the problem of a home for him. She had hoped that Grandad would come to her rescue, but he only talked to James about giving the old rabbit hutch a fresh coat of paint.

Now, three pairs of eyes rested on Mandy, Gran's puzzled, James's desperate, and Grandad's twinkling with amusement.

'You see, Gran, it's Humbug . . .' And as soon as she said his name, Mandy was off. She told her grandmother about the badger-diggers and Humbug's missing family, about the health and safety rules at Animal Ark, and about the lack of space at James's house. It was all Mrs Hope could do to stop the flow.

'So where do I come into all this?' she asked, with a little smile. And Mandy knew that Gran knew what they were going to ask. But to her surprise, it was James who spoke.

'Mrs Hope,' he said, very quietly, 'your basement is just the place for Humbug. He needs a quiet, dark, warm home, where he can get strong and healthy, before he goes back to the woods. Please would you let him stay in the basement – just for a while?' James turned bright pink and looked down at the table.

There was a pause so silent that they could hear the sparrows chattering outside.

Then: 'Well, I don't like the idea of a wild animal in the house. It might upset Smoky,' said Gran. 'But, after such a nice, polite request, how can I refuse?'

'Oh, thank you, Gran, thank you!' Mandy was back at the table, hugging and kissing her grandmother. Mr Hope was beaming at them both. James was already on his feet.

'I'll go and fetch him,' he said. 'And thank you very much, Mrs Hope.'

'Hey – wait for me. I want to carry Humbug back to his new home too,' laughed Mandy.

They ran down the lane back to Animal Ark, where they told Mandy's mother not to bother with the animal sanctuary and James rang his parents to tell them he'd be late. Then, together

they carried Humbug in the travelling cage, back up the lane to his new home in Lilac Cottage.

James lifted the sleeping badger out of his cage and settled him into the straw in the old rabbit hutch. Humbug merely stirred, snuggled into his new bed and slept on.

'Well,' said Gran, quite satisfied that the little creature was in no position to terrorise Smoky, 'we often have a hedgehog in the greenhouse and even moles in the lawn, but it's the first time we've had a badger in the basement!'

Five

On the first day of the half-term holiday, Mandy woke early. She opened her bedroom window wide and leaned dreamily on the sill, looking out over Animal Ark. She could hear the familiar sounds of hens from a nearby farm, and the cows murmuring as they came down from the meadow to be milked.

Mandy breathed deeply; the air was mild and damp, the clouded sky pearl grey. It would rain soon, she thought. And suddenly she was wide awake. Grandad had warned her that the tracks round the badger sett would be washed away by rain. If she wanted to get her evidence, she'd have to get moving!

* * *

'May I borrow your camera, Dad?' Mandy asked at breakfast.

'Hmm? Pass the marmalade, please.' Mr Hope was deep in thought, planning the day's calls.

'Dad! The camera – may I borrow it, please?' Mandy repeated slowly and loudly. 'And you've given up marmalade,' she reminded him.

Adam Hope groaned; he was always trying to lose weight. 'You can have the camera if I can have the marmalade,' he bargained.

Emily Hope laughed at the two of them. 'Well, that won't do either of you any good,' she said. She turned to Mandy. 'There's no film in the camera,' she explained. 'I can get you one in town later on today.'

Mandy sighed; one of the disadvantages of living in the country was the lack of shops. The McFarlanes kept their shop and post office stocked with everything from Coke to beefburgers but they didn't sell films. And by the time Mrs Hope got back from town, the rain would surely have started. So that was the end of that little plan, Mandy thought.

Her mind was already working on plan number two – James. She stood up and pushed her chair back sharply. 'I have to go – there's Humbug to

see to.' And she shot out before anyone could
protest.

James was already in the basement when Mandy
arrived. Humbug was scurrying about in his
travelling cage whilst James cleaned the hutch.
Mandy filled up the bowl with rabbit pellets and
took the feeding-bottle out of the wire mesh at
the front of the hutch. Simon had advised them
to use a bottle because badgers hate mess in
their cages and Humbug was a very sloppy drinker!

'I'll hold Humbug while he drinks his Vita-milk,'
she said.

James pushed his glasses up on his nose and
looked through them at Mandy, very seriously. 'I've
been talking to Walter Pickard,' he said. 'He says
we mustn't play with the badger, or even pick him
up.'

'Why not?'

'It'll muddle him.' James explained. 'We don't
want him to be friendly with humans when he goes
back home to the woods.' James looked anxious.
'We'll have to find a new sett for him,' he said.
'Somewhere far away from Piper's Wood.'

'Why?' asked Mandy.

'Well, I've been thinking,' said James. 'You know

whose land borders Piper's Wood?'

'No, whose?'

'Sam Western's!' said James.

And Mandy knew exactly what he meant. Sam Western would use any method possible to keep his land free of what he called 'vermin'. They both knew he'd tried to poison one of Lydia Fawcett's goats when it trespassed on his property. He was quite capable of flushing out badgers. But how? Mandy wondered. What about the tyre marks? To Mandy they looked quite worn and Sam Western would never leave worn tyres on his van. Unless he didn't want it known that he was in the woods and he used someone else's van?

Mandy looked at Humbug, then at James's tense face. This was just the right moment to tell him of her plan.

'Well, there may be something we can do,' she said slowly. 'You remember those tracks in the loose soil up in the woods?'

James nodded.

'Well, if we could trace the vehicle that made them . . .'

'But they could have come from anybody's van,' said James.

'Not these tyres,' Mandy assured him. 'They're

quite worn in parts. It should be easy to recognise them.'

'There must be lots of farmers riding around on worn tyres,' James pointed out.

'But not always in the same pattern,' replied Mandy. 'If we did some drawings of the tracks, we can keep a check on all the vans around here.'

James shook his head. 'We could never draw them accurately enough,' he said. 'And anyway, I can't come out this afternoon. We've got a family gathering – aunts and uncles to tea and all that. I've promised to show my cousin how to use his new computer game.'

He opened the travelling cage and tipped Humbug back into his hutch. The little badger snuffled round for his pellets and sat scrunching happily. Mandy watched him, gloomily. Plan number two dismissed! Sighing, she filled the bottle with the vitamin-milk powder and shook it up to mix it.

'Takes a bit of mixing,' she explained. 'You have to give it a good shake or the powder separates and it all goes chalky.' She held up the bottle in the dim light.

James watched her shaking the mixture.

'Plaster!' he said suddenly. 'That's what you need.'

'What?'

'To make plaster casts of the tracks in the wood.'

Mandy still looked puzzled so James explained. 'It's a way of checking animal tracks; we did it in environmental studies in the junior school. You make a mix of plaster of Paris, press it over the tracks, let it set, pull it off and, there you are, a perfect imprint!'

Mandy beamed. 'James, you're a genius!' she cried. 'We can go straight up there now. We'll need water – I can bring that in the bottle on my bike. You go and get the powder . . .'

'Where from?'

'Well, haven't you got some?'

'No, I told you – it was way back, when I was in the junior school . . .'

'Oh, James, what shall we do? We must get some sort of record of those tracks today; if it rains they'll all be washed away and we'll lose our evidence.'

They stood, deep in thought. Only the sound of the little badger, grinding at the mesh on his cage, disturbed the silence. James picked up the feeding-bottle, pushed it through the mesh and fixed it with a couple of rubber bands. Humbug stretched his neck and started to suck the tube at the end of the bottle.

'Oh, isn't he cute?' exclaimed Mandy. 'Mum says she'll call and give him a check-up later on. She'll be too busy just now: surgery's always packed on Saturday mornings . . .'

She broke off and looked at James.

'The surgery – of course!' she exclaimed. 'My parents sometimes use plaster to set broken limbs. I bet I can find some plaster of Paris at home.' Mandy turned to go. 'I'll fetch some then get straight off to Piper's Wood.'

'Hang on!' James hesitated. It was never easy to tell Mandy she couldn't do something. 'It's a bit tricky,' he said. 'My first few casts were useless; I didn't use enough powder.'

'So, what's the recipe?' Mandy pulled a chewed up Biro from her jeans pocket and prepared to write on her hand.

'I don't really know. I think a lot depends on the dampness in the air and on the state of the earth . . .' James sighed, heavily, trying to remember the details.

Mandy groaned. It all sounded very complicated and she was getting impatient.

'Tell you what,' said James. 'If you can be up at

the sett in half an hour I'll meet you there. But we'll have to be quick; Mum'll want me back for lunch – all those visitors, you know.'

Mandy grinned sympathetically. 'I'll be there,' she promised. 'Complete with plaster cast kit!'

'Plaster of Paris? What on earth for?' Mr Hope asked.

Mandy hesitated. She didn't want to tell lies to her father but, on the other hand, if she told him that she was on the track of catching a badger-killer he'd certainly forbid it.

'Er . . . I'm going to help James make plaster casts of some tracks,' she said, perfectly truthfully.

Her father laughed. 'You? You're not usually keen on tracking. What's come over you?'

Mandy, who couldn't think of an explanation right then, blushed and shook her head.

'It's not tracking I'm interested in, it's badgers,' she said. 'Since we got Humbug, you know . . .'

Well, that was certainly true!

'Go on.' Mr Hope grinned and ruffled her short blonde hair gently. 'The plaster powder's in the office. Help yourself to a small pack.'

'Oh, thanks, Dad!' Mandy leapt up to hug him and shot out of the door, almost knocking over her mother as she passed. 'Sorry, Mum – in a hurry!'

And she was gone.

Mandy pushed hard on her pedals; it was tough going uphill on the bridle-path through the woods but quicker than scrambling through the undergrowth like last time. She hoped James had managed to get away. What would she do if he hadn't? Well, she knew the answer to that; she'd just have to get on with the job all on her own.

But as she turned off the track into the clearing James's dog, Blackie, came bounding up to greet her.

'Hello, boy!' she said, dismounting before he could knock her off her bike. 'Have you brought James out for a walk?'

'Only a quick one!' came James's answer. 'Have you brought all the stuff?'

Mandy nodded. 'I even borrowed a plastic bowl to mix it in.'

'Great. Let's get on, then. I've found a few good ones close to the sett.'

The next few minutes were exciting. Mandy mixed the powder and water to a smooth, thick paste and watched with interest as James pressed it gently into the best of the tracks. After that, there was nothing more to do except to wait – and to keep Blackie from treading in the stuff!

Eventually, James looked at his watch. 'Twenty minutes – we'll have to risk it; I'm due home any time now.' He bent to peer at the plaster and tested it with his finger. 'This one's just about ready,' he announced. 'Did you bring anything to wrap them in?'

Mandy dived into her cycle bag and triumphantly waved a clutch of plastic bags she'd noticed hanging in the barn. James carefully lifted the first cast and placed it on the plastic bag.

'Leave it to dry a bit longer,' he told Mandy. 'I'll get the other two.'

He moved a bit further off and Mandy sat guarding the finished cast. She was so busy admiring it that she didn't notice Blackie running back and forth to the bridle-path, whining. It was only when he broke into fierce barks that she looked up.

There was a man standing at the edge of the clearing, watching them. Mandy picked up the plaster cast, thrust it into the bag and pushed it behind her. Then she stood up and called Blackie to heel. The man moved forwards a step or two. Blackie growled gently.

'He's quite a guard dog,' the man said. Now that he was closer, Mandy could see his face was ruddy, as if he spent a lot of time outdoors, and he had a short, grizzled beard. He was wearing a green body-warmer and a battered tweedy hat. 'What's he up to?' he demanded, nodding in the direction of James.

'He's . . . er . . . collecting,' said Mandy, thinking furiously. 'Tracks,' she added. 'They say there are badgers round here, you know,' she went on, brightly.

'Not any more there aren't.'

Mandy thought he sounded pleased about that. 'He thought he might pick up some prints.' She smiled nervously, praying that James would hear them talking and hide his casts. For all they knew this man might be one of the badger-diggers himself! As if to share her suspicions, Blackie gave another growl.

'Lovely dog, that,' the man said. But he didn't move any closer. 'Is he yours?'

'No. He belongs to James – over there.'

The man nodded. 'You want to watch him in these 'ere woods. Friend of mine lost a dog round here only a few days ago.'

'Lost a dog? How awful!' Mandy said. It was bad enough to have an animal die, but to lose one was even worse. You could never know what had happened to it. Mandy shivered at the thought of anything like that happening to Blackie.

She turned to look at the man who coughed gruffly and continued to stare at Blackie. Nervously, Mandy looked on. He had a friend who'd lost a dog, he said. And he seemed to know that the badgers had gone. What if he and his friend had lost the dog when they were looking for badgers? Digging for badgers?

'Hey, Mandy, can you bring me a bag, please?'

James's voice interrupted her speculations. And for once, Mandy was grateful.

'I'll have to go and help him now,' said Mandy. ' 'Bye!' She called Blackie and went quickly over to James.

'Shove those casts in the bag and hide them!' she commanded as soon as she was within earshot.

'No, leave them out to dry a bit longer. I'll have to get back but you can wait another ten minutes, just to make sure.'

'Just put them in the bag!' Mandy repeated. 'And give them to me!'

James looked up at her. 'What's the matter?' he asked.

'Over there – near the bridle-path,' Mandy jerked her head in the direction of the man.

James stood up and looked across the clearing. 'What?' he asked.

'That man – can't you see? He might be one of the diggers.' Mandy turned to look once more. The man had gone. And she remembered her promise to her grandfather. She wasn't going to linger in the woods on her own.

'Come on, we'll have to risk the plaster being dry. I'll pack them very carefully into my saddle-bag and dry them out at home.'

'But there's nobody there, Mandy.'

'There was; I spoke to him and he was very interested in what you were doing. I let him think you were collecting badger tracks. And he knew the badgers had gone.'

'Half the county knows that now. That doesn't make him a criminal,' said James.

'Whatever he is, I don't want to be left in the woods on my own with him around,' said Mandy. 'Now, come on, help me pack my bag, then you can get back to your cousin's computer game!'

Mandy rode back slowly and carefully, steering round all the stomach-jerking bumps she usually enjoyed. When she got back to Animal Ark, she took her treasures up to her room and set them out in the sun on the windowsill. Then she went in search of lunch.

'Had an instructive morning with James?' Mr Hope enquired. 'Soup and salad do you? We'll cook tonight when Mum's back from town.' He poured Mrs Hope's best home-made leek and potato soup into two bowls, fetched garlic bread from the oven and sat with Mandy at the kitchen table.

'Did you get some good tracks?' he asked,

watching longingly as Mandy spread butter thickly over her bread.

Mandy smiled and passed him a packet of crispbreads, but not the butter. 'Oh, yes, Dad,' she said. 'We got some terrific tracks!'

Six

'Shall I hold him while you clean out the cage?' Mandy asked James. It was a few days after they'd rescued Humbug and she was longing to have a chance to touch him and examine him closely.

'Nay, lass, you mustn't do that!' Walter Pickard had come to Lilac Cottage to see how the little badger was getting along. 'He's got to go back into the woods, d'you see. You don't want to make a pet of him.'

Mandy sighed, though she knew he was right; Walter Pickard was the village expert on wildlife and he'd given them some very useful advice.

'You're doing very nicely with the little 'un,' he

told them today. 'Coming on a treat, he is. You're giving him a good mixed diet, like I told you?'

'Oh yes, Mr Pickard,' James assured him. Walter had told them that even very young badgers like a bit of meat as well as their mother's milk. So every morning now they fed the cub on rabbit pellets mixed with raw mince.

'And you're keeping him nice and clean, I see.' Walter peered into the hutch and nodded his approval. 'Badgers do like to keep their places clean, you know.'

Mandy and James cleaned out the hutch, filled up his water bottle and then walked down the lane with Walter, leaving Humbug quite alone in the dark, peaceful basement. And although Mandy knew that was the right thing to do, it didn't stop her wanting to make friends with the little badger.

'Shall I take Patch for a little run while you clean out the kennel?' she asked Simon, later that same morning. They were standing in front of the terrier's kennel. 'She's getting better every day now.'

She was right; Patch's wounds had almost healed, leaving only faint stitch marks, and she trotted around quite confidently on three legs and a plaster. She was in an outdoor kennel, which was not a kennel at all, more a concrete run, completely enclosed in strong wire mesh and with a warm, cosy hut at one end. Patch was quite happy there, with enough room to move around, lots of good food and a comfortable bed in the hut.

'An outing will do her good now that she's moving so well,' Mandy said.

Simon shook his head. 'She's not your dog, Mandy. You can't go taking other people's dogs out without their permission.'

'But she needs the exercise.'

'She's getting quite enough at the moment, with her leg in plaster.' Simon moved on to the next run where a huge Great Dane was sprawled, looking very sorry for himself.

'Would you like to help me feed this one?' he asked.

But Mandy shook her head; it was Patch she wanted and if Simon wouldn't let her take the dog out, she'd take a mug of coffee to her mother and try to persuade her.

She found her in the office, sorting out Jean's muddles. 'Thanks, love, I'm ready for this.' Mrs Hope took the coffee and went on checking the appointments schedule.

But Mandy perched on the edge of the desk. 'Mum, you know that terrier?'

'Hmm?' Mrs Hope didn't raise her head.

But Mandy went on, 'Well, she's a lot better now, so I think I ought to take her out to exercise that leg.'

Mrs Hope looked up and reached for her coffee. She sipped it, slowly, smiling at Mandy over the rim of the mug. 'Yes, well, I think you're right,' she agreed.

Mandy beamed. 'You do? Then can you please tell Simon to let me take her out.'

'No, wait! I mean you're right about the dog being ready to move. She's not fully recovered yet, but there's no need for her to stay here, so long as Mr Bonser is careful with her.' She shuffled through some computer print-outs in front of her. 'Oh dear, Jean's not got the bill ready so I can't send it out. I'll have a talk to him when he comes in. He can only take the dog home if he understands how to treat her.' Mrs Hope picked up the internal phone. 'Jean? Can you pop in here a moment?' She looked at Mandy, expecting her to leave.

Mandy wandered back to the house, appalled. What had she done? Got Patch sent home, that's what. She frowned at the idea. Would Mr Bonser take care of Patch properly? He didn't even take care of his own van properly – it was worse than Simon's. And Mandy wasn't at all sure he'd listen to her mother's advice, as he'd been so rude on his previous visit to Animal Ark.

She recollected her father's words on that occasion: 'People are sometimes rude when they're nervous.' Perhaps if she went to see Mr Bonser on his home ground, he wouldn't be so nervous; perhaps he'd listen to her and she could make sure he'd treat Patch properly.

Mandy rushed off upstairs. Half-term wasn't going to be so dull after all! She knew Mr Bonser's farm; after all she'd filled in his card that day. Old Dyke Farm was a pig farm out towards the Beacon – on the way to Upper Welford Hall, where Sam Western lived.

As she pedalled off down the lane, Mandy suddenly thought of James. He always enjoyed a bike ride and he might even be useful back-up if Mr Bonser wouldn't listen to her. Mandy clicked up a gear and raced down the hill to James's house.

But James's delight in being invited to go for a bike ride soon turned to doubt when he discovered where they were going. 'You said he was rude and a bit rough,' he objected.

'Well, that might have been because he was worried,' explained Mandy. 'People sometimes sound cross when they're really just frightened,' she added, sounding more certain than she felt.

'But what if he's not even there?' said James.

'Oh, we'll just cycle up and look round. If anybody stops us we'll say we have a message for Mr Bonser – which we have.'

James couldn't deny this so together they cycled out of the village and up the hill. The main road was smooth and lovely to ride, but the narrow, twisty drive up to Mr Bonser's pig farm was in a poor condition; they bumped and banged up it, twisting and turning to avoid the worst potholes.

'If I get a puncture you can jolly well mend it,' said James, puffing and complaining all the way.

'All right – I promise!' Mandy herself was beginning to have doubts.

'Don't suppose you even have a repair kit in your bag,' James went on grumbling. Suddenly he dropped into a deep hole. 'Ow!' He stalled and fell off his bike.

Mandy stopped and dismounted in case he needed any help. But she suddenly heard the sound of a car engine. It was coming down the drive towards them.

'Quick, get up!' Mandy dropped her bike down into the ditch and rushed over to pick up James and push him to safety on the overgrown grass verge. Mandy peered through the long grass and saw that Mr Bonser was driving the van.

'Oh, no. He's gone out now,' she said.

'Good – we can go home.' James scrambled up and brushed himself down.

'Wait a minute, this is a good chance to have a look round the farm,' said Mandy.

'What for?'

Mandy hesitated; she had no idea but she didn't like to think they'd come all that way for nothing.

'You never know,' she said mysteriously. 'We might find out something about Mr Bonser.'

'I'm not cycling over those potholes again,' said James.

'OK, we'll walk.' And Mandy set off, leaving her bike hidden in the ditch. She knew that James would either wait for her or follow.

He followed.

Old Dyke Farm wasn't so much a farm as a sort of scrap-heap-cum-smallholding. Scattered about the yard in front of the small cottage were rusting machine parts, loose heaps of straw, piles of old motor tyres, lengths of timber, doors, even an old lavatory.

'What a mess!' said Mandy, surveying the scene.

'Being untidy's not a crime,' grinned James.

'No, but it's a funny sort of pig farm,' Mandy observed. 'I see no pigs!'

James sniffed. 'Nor smell any, either,' he said.

'Maybe he's gone bust?' They both knew that some local farmers were having a very difficult time just now.

Mandy frowned. 'Well, if he has he might be looking for new ways of making money. Come on, we might just find out what he's up to.'

'But what are we looking for?' asked James.

'I don't know – anything unusual – like a pig farm with no pigs.'

They went over to the piggeries, old concrete buildings now stripped and empty but securely locked, nevertheless. Mandy pulled at the first door but it wouldn't budge.

'There's nothing here, Mandy. Come on, let's go,' James said nervously. 'We shouldn't be poking about on somebody else's farm like this.'

'Oh, all right!' Mandy followed him along the

length of the piggeries, banging on each door as she passed.

At the last door she stopped. There was a faint sound coming from inside the sty. A sound of . . . whining, whimpering perhaps?

'There you are!' said Mandy, triumphant. 'Listen to that!'

They stood silent, listening hard. It certainly was a whimper, and a very faint, high-pitched squeaking.

'Pigs don't whimper,' said James. 'They squeal.'

'That's not pigs, it's dogs,' whispered Mandy.

'Oh, well, just the farm dogs, I expect.' James moved off.

'But they're locked in there – in the dark!' Mandy rushed after him. 'We can't leave them like that!'

James turned to her. 'Look, Mandy, plenty of farmers keep their dogs outside, in kennels, barns – boxes, for all I know. Mr Bonser will probably let them out when he comes back.'

'But if they're farm dogs he'd have left them on guard,' Mandy argued. 'They were crying to be let out – and to be fed, if I'm not mistaken. They sounded hungry, James!'

But James wouldn't even stop to answer; he was

anxious to get off Mr Bonser's land. Mandy gave a worried glance back at the piggeries, hesitated, then raced to catch up with James. Silently, they picked up their bikes and pushed them to the end of Mr Bonser's drive. They were just coming up to the main road when the ramshackle blue van turned in to the drive.

'Oh, help, it's him!' James moaned.

'Good!' Mandy was quite excited. 'Now, I'll do the talking while you get the registration number – OK?'

'But . . .'

Too late, James saw the van slow down and pull alongside Mandy, who was actually waving it down!

'Hi, Mr Bonser,' Mandy called cheerfully.

He slid back his window and peered down at her. 'What are you doing on my land?' he demanded.

Mandy waggled a hand behind her back to indicate that James should stay behind the van. 'Er . . . You are Mr Bonser, aren't you?' she asked, playing for time.

'Who wants to know?' he asked suspiciously. 'If you kids have been up to any mischief on my land I'll . . .'

'Oh, no, we just came to . . . to deliver a message, and you weren't there, so we were just leaving.'

'Message? Who from?' Mr Bonser suddenly looked anxious.

'From the vet – at Animal Ark,' Mandy explained. 'Remember me, Mr Bonser? I was there when you brought your dog in.'

Mr Bonser shook his head. 'My dog's here with me,' he said, jerking his head towards the back of the van.

Is it? thought Mandy. Then what were the other dogs doing, all shut up in a piggery? And who did Patch belong to? She glanced down and saw James, kneeling on the ground, peering at the battered number plate.

'Your injured terrier,' she reminded Mr Bonser. 'You brought her to Animal Ark.'

Mr Bonser seemed uneasy. 'Not my dog,' he said. 'Brought it in for somebody else.'

For a moment, Mandy was flooded with relief. Perhaps Patch wouldn't have to go back to Old Dyke Farm after all. 'Well, perhaps you could tell the owner his dog's nearly better.'

'And you've come all this way just to tell me that?' He glared at her in disbelief.

Mandy swallowed hard. 'Not just that, no. Er,

well . . . Mum says can you come and collect him,' she said, faintly, feeling terrible at betraying poor Patch. But she had to say something to explain her presence at Old Dyke Farm and the kind of heart-to-heart chat she'd planned didn't seem to be working. 'We need the kennel, you see, for another patient.'

Mr Bonser eyed her suspiciously. 'Oh, aye? And does your mum say who's going to foot the bill?'

Out of the corner of her eye, Mandy saw James getting up. 'Er . . . well, I suppose you'll have to discuss that with her,' she said, hurriedly. 'I must get back, now, I'll tell her I saw you. 'Bye!'

They leapt on to their bikes and pedalled hard without saying a word. When they reached the Fox and Goose crossroads they stopped, dropped their bikes on to the village green and flopped down on the bench beside them.

'Well – did you get the number?' Mandy asked.

James nodded. 'But what's it for?' he asked.

'I don't know,' Mandy admitted. 'I just thought it might be useful.' A thought struck her. 'Did you get a look at his tyres?' she asked.

He shook his head. 'Not specially,' he said. 'Why?'

Mandy shrugged. 'I just wondered whether

they'd match our plaster casts.'

'Well, I did notice the back tyres are very worn,' James admitted, cautiously. 'But that's as far as it goes.'

Mandy refused to be put down. 'So, we'll take it just a bit further,' she said.

'How?'

'Easy! Next time we see Mr Bonser's van we'll check his tyres against our casts.'

'Oh yeah? Like when? I've never seen him around Welford.'

Mandy bit hard on a grass stalk and turned away from James. 'He's got to come to Animal Ark to collect Patch,' she said. 'And he's bound to make trouble about the bill. While the discussion goes on, I can check his tyres against the casts.'

'I thought you didn't want the dog to go back to Mr Bonser?' James said.

Mandy sniffed. 'He might not get her back if we can prove he was involved in the badger-digging.'

They were both quiet for a moment. Mandy was weighing up the odds against Mr Bonser being caught and Patch being rescued.

'He might not come down to get the dog,' James said suddenly.

'Oh yes he will; Mum's sending for him.'

'But he might turn up when you're not there,' James pointed out.

He was right; they'd be back at school next week. There must be another way . . .

'Simon!' she said suddenly.

'Where?' James looked round.

'No – Simon's at Animal Ark most of the time; he can do it.'

'Do you think he will?'

'He will if you tell him about the badger-digging; he's a wildlife nut like you.'

James stood and drew himself up as tall as he could. 'The word is "enthusiast", not "nut", Mandy. You know sometimes I wonder why I'm your friend!'

Mandy grinned. 'Because you're a wildlife enthusiast!' she said. 'Now, let's go home and find Simon – and some dinner!' she said. 'Race you!'

Seven

Simon was an enthusiast too. Once he'd heard their story, he agreed to keep a look out for Mr Bonser.

'While Mrs Hope shows him how to look after the dog, I'll make a rubbing from the front tyre,' he said. 'Then you can match it against your casts.' He winked at Mandy and slipped on his white coat, ready for surgery. 'You can rely on me,' he promised.

So the next day, Mandy skipped into the kitchen for breakfast, feeling delighted with herself. Everything was going to plan. She had the plaster casts, Simon was going to make rubbings of the tyres and James had the registration number of the van. All they had to do was to put the lot together and that would be the end of the badger-digging. And if Mr Bonser had left Patch to be attacked, well, that might just be the end of his dog-owning career. Humming happily to herself, Mandy shook a huge heap of cornflakes into her bowl.

And then the phone rang.

'It's for you!' Dad called, on his way through the hall. 'It's James.'

Good! thought Mandy as she picked up the receiver. James must have some important news about Mr Bonser, at last.

'Mandy, he's got away!' She could hear James's voice trembling even over the phone.

Mandy's thoughts were still on Mr Bonser. 'What do you mean?' she asked eagerly. 'Where to?' If Mr Bonser had disappeared, perhaps he'd warned the badger-diggers off and both Humbug and Patch would be safe.

'I don't know – I just heard from your grandad. I'll meet you down there – right away!' And James banged the phone down.

For a moment Mandy didn't move. It was a well-known fact that you couldn't do anything secret in Welford, but how on earth had Grandad heard about their visit to Mr Bonser? Mandy shivered: she had a feeling there was trouble about, though she couldn't quite work out what. Well, she'd better get over to Lilac Cottage straight away.

She took the short cut, over the back lawn, through the hedge and down the narrow path to the back garden of Lilac Cottage, practising the route to take on mornings before school the following week, since Humbug would need feeding.

Humbug! Mandy stood quite still in the middle of the path. Suddenly James's message made sense; it wasn't Mr Bonser who'd escaped. It was Humbug! That's why Grandad had rung James. The badger had got out and was on the loose – maybe going back to Piper's Wood.

With new-found energy she tore down the path, vaulted over the gate and raced across her grandparents' garden. James was already at the basement, his ear pressed to the door, listening intently.

'James!' Mandy ran up to him. 'What's happened?'

'Shh!' He just waggled a hand to her. 'Listen!'

Mandy pressed her ear to the door; she heard

only her own breathing, being rather puffed out after her run. There was no other sound.

'I can't hear anything,' she whispered.

'No, he's probably sleeping now.' James moved off, away from the basement, beckoning Mandy to follow him round the side of the cottage, to the kitchen door.

'Your gran's in quite a state,' he warned her.

She certainly was!

'He was up half the night rampaging about,' she told them. 'I thought we had burglars . . . Tom would insist on going down . . . it was quite frightening until we realised it was all that badger's fault.'

And James explained that Humbug had escaped from the hutch during the night, and gone hunting in the basement.

Mandy breathed a sigh of relief. 'Well, he must still be in there,' she said. 'We've only got to find him and put him back.'

But James shook his head doubtfully, looking rather gloomily at Mandy's grandmother.

Anyone could see she was quite upset, and Mandy couldn't blame her. She hadn't been happy about having the badger in the house from the start.

Mandy moved over to hug her grandmother. 'We'll make sure he's locked up safely when we get him,' she promised. 'It won't happen again.'

'It certainly won't,' said Gran. 'He's just got to go!'

Mandy decided this was not the time to argue. 'Where's Grandad?' she asked.

'He's looking for the key to the basement door.'

'No!' James almost shouted. 'We can't go in that way. As soon as the door's opened, Humbug'll be off like a shot across the garden.'

Gran shook her head. 'There's another door into the basement, from the hall. Even if the animal does escape it'll only get as far as the hall and you can catch him easily.'

As soon as Grandad came in with the key, they left Gran shut firmly in the kitchen with the kitten and went into the hall. Mr Hope unlocked the little door to the basement and Mandy and James stood by to catch whatever came rushing out.

But nothing did. The door creaked open but all was quiet. Very quickly, James led the way down the steps. Mandy followed and Grandad pulled the door shut as he came in last.

Only the sound of their breathing and the boiler hissing gently to itself disturbed the utter silence.

They stood still until their eyes became accustomed to the darkness, then they began to look around them. Mandy moved over to the hutch. Its door was still closed but even in that dim light she could see where the mesh had frayed away from the front. Humbug had obviously found a weak spot in the old wire and worked away at it.

'He's chewed his way out,' she whispered. 'He must have been desperate.' She thought of the little cub trying to get back to his home in the woods, and to his family who no longer lived there. Mandy sniffed loudly.

'Shh!' James hissed. But nothing stirred.

Grandad spoke very gently. 'I don't think we'll disturb him. Badgers are night-time creatures and he's been up and about for many hours. He'll sleep now, all day, I shouldn't wonder.'

'But where is he?' James was prowling about the dimly-lit basement, peering into corners, even up on shelves.

'He could be anywhere,' said Mr Hope. They all looked around the junk-filled basement. There were so many places for a small animal to curl up in: rolls of carpet, cardboard boxes, piles of gardening magazines, rows of paint tins, even the base of a spare bed propped against a wall. Where could they start looking?

'We'll have to wait until he's hungry and comes out,' said James. 'And keep watch.'

'But he might be asleep all day!' protested Mandy, forgetting to keep her voice quiet.

'Shh!' her grandfather reminded her. 'We'll take turns, and put food down, so that when he does wake he'll stop to eat.'

Lucky Humbug, thought Mandy, feeling suddenly hungry herself. She remembered her uneaten bowl of cornflakes on the breakfast table, and all the things she had meant to do that morning: feed her rabbits, clean them out, check up on the patients in the hospital, call to see Patch . . .

Suddenly struck by an idea, Mandy spoke out loud. 'Patch!' she said, 'that's who we need.'

'Mandy!' James whispered. 'If you can't be quiet go and do something useful.'

'Right!' said Mandy. 'You just hang on in here. I'll be back very soon.'

She ran lightly up the steps, slipped back through the hall door and was off home in a flash.

When she returned she brought a flask of coffee,

a bag of buttered scones – and Patch! Getting the coffee and scones had proved much easier than getting the dog.

'You can't take a dog out without the owner's permission,' Mrs Hope had told her when Mandy had asked to borrow Patch. 'You know Dad's rules.' But she had made a flask of coffee and buttered the scones for the badger watchers.

'Good luck,' she said 'I do hope you find the little badger. But don't go bothering Gran.'

When Mandy appealed to Simon, however, he agreed that a lost badger cub was more important than broken rules.

'But for heaven's sake have her back before the end of surgery,' he said. 'Whether you find the badger or not – right?'

'Right,' Mandy had promised.

Simon checked Patch's leg plaster, put on a collar and a lead, and told Mandy to carry the dog round to Lilac Cottage.

'She can walk about the basement, but that's all,' he said. 'Give her time to get used to the place before you put her down. Keep her on the lead. And as soon as that badger moves pick the dog up quick! We don't want any more wounds!'

* * *

James was horrified at the idea of setting the sharp little terrier to sniff Humbug out, but Mr Hope agreed with Mandy – it was the best way to find Humbug quickly. So he found a piece of old blanket and brought out the travelling cage.

'As soon as the badger moves out, you throw the blanket over him, Mandy picks up the dog, and I'll hold the cage. James, you pop him in, and there we are. Right?'

The other two nodded. Even in the dim light of the basement, Mandy could see James's white, tense face. She could feel Patch shivering in her arms, and for a moment she wondered whether they were doing the right thing. What if Patch set upon Humbug? And what if Humbug fought back? Poor Patch had suffered enough wounds from some fight or other.

But Patch made the first move, wriggling in Mandy's arms. Gripping the lead hard, Mandy carefully lowered the dog to the ground and followed her. The first thing she did was to squat on the concrete floor and make a puddle!

'Oh, dear, I'm so sorry, Grandad!' murmured Mandy. 'I'll scrub the floor when all this is over.'

Grandad smiled. 'She's just establishing her

territory,' he said. 'It may even be useful if Humbug gets the scent.'

But, wherever he was, Humbug was not getting any sort of scent. Patch hopped around happily, sniffing the walls and stopping for a long time to breathe in the fresh air from under the garden door. She obviously would have preferred her first outing to have been out there!

'Take her over to the hutch,' James suggested. 'Then she'll get Humbug's scent.'

'That might frighten her,' said Mandy. 'Don't forget what some wild creature did to her.'

'You can always give her one of your cuddles,' grinned James. He was feeling happier now he'd had some food, and now that there was some hope of finding Humbug soon.

Mr Hope put the old hutch down on the floor and Mandy gently led Patch towards it. As soon as the dog sniffed the straw, she backed off, snarling, hackles raised, eyes wild. And as if that was some sort of signal, there came a shuffling from a dark corner of the room.

Patch turned her head, nose quivering, tail vertical, and faced Humbug, who was advancing towards his hutch. For one moment they eyed each other, lean bodies stretched and still, both

shivering. Then with a savage cry, Humbug threw himself across the floor!

Quick as a flash, Mandy bent and picked up the terrier, holding her close in her arms and stroking her head. James, meantime, threw the old blanket over Humbug and held him close, well-wrapped but still struggling. Mr Hope held the travelling cage and James shoved Humbug in, blanket and all. Snap! The door was clipped down, the cage put up on the shelf and that was that.

The three of them grinned at one another. Now all they had to do was to face Gran.

* * *

'I'm sorry, Mandy, but I can't take another night like last night.' Gran pushed a mug of hot chocolate across the kitchen table. 'That animal has to go.'

James sipped his chocolate and looked gloomy. Mandy's grandfather nibbled a digestive biscuit thoughtfully.

'But it won't be another night like last night, Gran!' said Mandy. 'We'll get another hutch – a good one, one that Humbug can't escape from. He'll be quite safe.' She had no idea where they'd find another hutch; that was just the next problem.

'That's as may be, but have you thought why the little creature was trying to escape?' Gran looked round the table.

'He wanted to go hunting,' said James.

'He wanted to go home,' said Mrs Hope.

There was a silence. They all realised the truth of this. But how could they set Humbug free to live alone in a sett that had already been dug out?

'He hasn't got a home,' said James, sadly. 'And he hasn't got a family to look after him.'

Mandy sniffed. She turned her head away and looked across the kitchen. Quite worn out by her morning's work, Patch had settled herself in the kitten's basket by the cooker; the kitten was snuggled on her back, fast asleep.

'Look at that,' Mandy said. 'Humbug's only a kitten, too, you know, Gran. You wouldn't want to turn Smoky out, now would you?'

Gran shook her head slowly. 'But a badger is a wild animal,' she said quietly.

'And Humbug will go back to the woods as soon as we can arrange it,' said James.

'As soon as this afternoon?' Gran asked him.

And James shook his head.

Mr Hope stood up. 'Talking about this afternoon,' he said, looking over to his wife, 'hadn't we better be getting on with the packing?'

'Well, I don't know about that,' said Mandy's grandmother. 'Not after all this upset.'

'We were planning a trip in the camper van,' Mr Hope explained. 'Just a day or two, to get Smoky used to it.'

'But he's had enough excitement for one weekend,' said Gran. 'And so have I!'

Mr Hope smiled at her. 'Now look at that kitten,' he said. 'He'll be ready for anything after a rest. Just like you,' he added.

Mrs Hope laughed. 'Well, they say a change is as good as a rest, Tom.'

'So you'll come?' he asked her.

She nodded. 'Of course we'll have to take the cat basket and the travelling box, and several tins of cat food and . . .' She got up, ready to bustle away.

Mandy suddenly realised what her grandfather was doing. 'But Gran, if you're away this weekend, Humbug won't disturb you, will he?'

Gran stood still, looked at Mandy, then over to Mr Hope. 'Well, I suppose you've done it again, you two,' she smiled. 'I can't complain about being disturbed if I'm a hundred miles away, can I?'

Mandy grinned at James. James beamed over his glasses at Mrs Hope.

'Oh, thank you,' he said. 'I'll make sure he's quite secure this time.'

'And you must make sure you start preparing to let him go,' said Mr Hope. 'Dorothy's right, you know. He is pining for the woods.'

James nodded. 'I'll go and see Walter Pickard and get some advice. We'll set him loose quite soon,' he promised.

'Right! Now if we're to set off at all today, we must get on, Tom.' Mrs Hope started to collect the mugs.

'Oh, I'll clear up,' Mandy jumped up. 'Come on, James. I'll wash, you dry.'

Mr Hope looked down at the cat basket. 'I think you'd better get this dog back to Animal Ark,' he reminded her. 'And ask our Adam to bring a secure hutch round, too.'

A few minutes later, Mandy walked down the lane to Animal Ark, Patch snuggled in her arms. Back at Lilac Cottage, Humbug was snuggled in his mended cage, and everything was all right once more. She started to sing a lullaby to Patch as she made her way up the path to the red door of Animal Ark.

But she didn't finish the song. She stood in the middle of the path and looked at the van, parked right in the middle of the surgery carpark. A shabby, blue van.

Mr Bonser had taken her at her word. He'd come to collect his dog!

Eight

Mandy hesitated. No one had seen her; she could just turn round and run away with Patch. For a moment she even believed it. And then she came to her senses. Patch still had her plaster on, still needed treatment, and Mandy would never deprive her of that. Sighing, she walked slowly towards the surgery.

'Psst! Mandy – over here!'

It was Simon's voice. But there was no sign of Simon.

'Where are you?' she asked, quietly.

'Other side of the van – quick, before anyone sees you!'

Mandy slid round the back of the van and round the other side, hidden from the surgery. She heard a strange, rustling sound down by the near-side wheel. Looking down, she saw Simon busily rubbing a bit of wax crayon up and down on a paper pressed to the tyre.

'Where on earth have you been?' he asked without pausing. 'No, there's no time to tell me. Is the badger safe?'

Mandy nodded.

'Good. He's the only one who is.' Simon nodded up at the van. 'I had to tell your mum where the dog was, Mandy. I'm sorry. She's been trying to keep Mr Bonser busy in the office and Jean's been filling him with coffee and shortbreads. Go on – take the dog back up to the kennels.'

'We can't let him take her,' she protested.

'He may not even want her,' Simon pointed out. 'Not after all the instructions your mum's been giving him. But if he goes up to the kennels and finds her missing, he'll go berserk. Now – go!'

Obeying the urgency in his tone, Mandy walked round the front of the van, then slipped quickly past the surgery and round to the kennels. It took only a moment to put Patch into hers, click the lock and leave her standing there, alone and rather forlorn.

Even as Mandy turned to go she heard them approaching. Mr Bonser was talking in a very loud voice.

'You've no right,' he was saying. 'No right at all!'

Mrs Hope's face was serious, but she forced a smile.

'I really can't release a sick animal unless I'm sure you know how to take care of her,' she replied. 'Otherwise you must leave her with me for a few days.'

'I'll decide that, missus,' he said. 'Just let me see that dog.'

He strode down the path towards the kennels, then stopped when he saw Mandy. 'What are you doing 'ere?' he asked.

Mandy looked past him to her mother. She wasn't sure how to play this one. 'Oh, Mr Bonser,' she said in an over-sweet tone. 'I was just saying good morning to your little dog.'

He grunted and pushed past her. Mandy moved to stand by her mother, who, for some reason, pulled Mandy towards her and began brushing at the front of her old, black T-shirt.

'Oh, Mandy, when will you learn to eat your

cornflakes without them slopping all down you?'
she said.

Mandy was puzzled; she hadn't even had time
for breakfast that morning and anyway, she never
slopped it down her front. She looked down as
her mother frantically scrubbed at her front,
shifting Patch's white hairs.

'Oh!' said Mandy, with sudden realisation. She
glanced at Mr Bonser, crouching now in front of
the kennel. 'Oh, it's all right, Mum, it's only my
old T-shirt.' But she nodded to her mother and
mouthed her thanks.

'Come on out, you silly great dog!' Mr Bonser
was calling through the wire. He turned accusingly
to Mrs Hope. 'It's gone in,' he said. 'Won't come
out.'

And Mandy could just see a pair of little shiny
eyes peeping from the hut at the back of the run.

'Come on out,' he bellowed once more.

The dog merely lifted a lip in a snarl and
cowered back into the hut.

'You see, she's not ready to be taken out yet,'
Mrs Hope told him. 'She needs to rest a few more
days.'

But Mr Bonser shook his head, rather
desperately.

'I don't care what she needs,' he said. 'I need a dog.'

'Need?' Mrs Hope raised her eyebrows. 'What on earth could you need a little terrier like that for?' she asked.

There was a pause. Mr Bonser stood up, towering over both mother and daughter. 'Never you mind,' he muttered. 'That there's my dog and I'm taking it now!'

Mandy was puzzled; back at the farm, Mr Bonser had told her that the dog wasn't his but now he was claiming her as his own. She looked up at her mother, wondering whether to interfere. Better not, she decided. If anyone could face up to Mr Bonser, it was Emily Hope!

'Tell you what, Mr Bonser,' Mrs Hope spoke in a very reasonable tone. 'I'll keep the dog another day or two, just to keep an eye on her, at no extra cost to you. How does that strike you?' And she smiled her widest, most winning smile.

Mr Bonser stepped back, as if to ward off Emily Hope's charm. 'Strike me?' he said. 'It strikes me that you're kidnapping my dog!'

'Not at all, Mr Bonser,' Mrs Hope said coldly. 'I'm treating your dog for some rather unusual injuries.' There was no mistaking the threat in her voice.

Mr Bonser heard it. 'What do you mean?' he blustered.

'I mean that the dog has been badly treated: it's been in a very nasty fight with some animal or other but a healthy dog – a well-fed dog – would have recovered by now.' She drew herself up as tall as Bonser and looked him straight in the eye. 'In view of her general condition, I can't remove the plaster from her leg for a few days yet.'

Mr Bonser scowled. 'She can manage on three legs, can't she?'

Mrs Hope sighed. 'Yes,' she said. 'She can manage to hobble around, but she's not yet fit to go out. You can see for yourself she's still shocked and nervous.'

'No, I can't. Damned animal won't budge!'

Mrs Hope turned to Mandy. 'Could you persuade the dog to come out?' she asked, calmly.

Horrified, Mandy dropped her mother's hand and stepped back. Was she really going to hand Patch over to this man? But Mrs Hope merely nodded and urged her forward. With shaking fingers, Mandy clicked open the wire door and walked across to the hut.

'Patch!' she called, softly. 'Come on, Patch.'

She put her hand into the hut and tickled the

dog's ears. Patch licked her fingers and whined gently.

'Come on,' she murmured. 'I won't let him hurt you.' And she lifted the little terrier out.

'Well done, darling,' called her mother. 'Now, put her down on the ground, will you?'

Puzzled, Mandy knelt and put Patch gently on to the concrete floor. Immediately she hobbled back into Mandy's lap. Mandy looked back at her mother.

'Put her down again,' she said.

Mandy lifted the dog off her lap and gently put her on the ground. Patch looked round and hobbled a few steps. Then she caught sight of Mr Bonser and crouched on the concrete, shivering and snarling. Finally she turned and made a dive for Mandy's lap, pushed her muzzle right under Mandy's arm and hid her face, whimpering.

Mrs Hope turned to Mr Bonser. 'You see,' she said, gently. 'It's not only the physical wounds that have to heal. You must admit she's in no fit state to come back to work for you.'

'Who said anything about work?' he asked, suspiciously.

'You did. You said you needed a dog; I assumed you meant for ratting, or something . . .' Her words hung heavily between them.

Cuddling the terrified dog, Mandy looked in wonderment from Mr Bonser to her mother.

Suddenly the man turned. 'Tell you this much, missus,' he shouted. 'I'll leave it till tomorrow and if you don't release that dog then, I'll have the law on you.'

He pushed her roughly aside, strode down the path and jumped into his van. The ignition coughed several times before the engine started. Mandy hoped Simon had finished the tyre rubbings!

But Mr Bonser wasn't leaving yet. He thrust his head out of the van window. 'And you'll not get a penny off me!' He shouted. 'Not ever!' He revved the engine noisily, turned the lumbering vehicle round with a screech of tyres and shot down the drive, fast.

'Well, well, well,' murmured Mrs Hope. 'That was all rather interesting, wasn't it?' Suddenly she turned to Mandy. 'Right,' she ordered, briskly. 'Just leave the dog there, and let's go into the office. I think we need a little talk, don't you?'

Mandy hurriedly popped Patch back into the hut and followed her mother down the path between the kennels. She didn't like her mother's tone; there was going to be trouble right enough, and she was going to be in the middle of it! As they crossed the yard, the Land-rover pulled in, and Mr Hope dropped down from the driving seat, followed by James.

'Any chance of lunch for two hungry badger-tamers?' asked Mr Hope.

'Could you wait a moment, please, Adam?' Mrs Hope asked him. 'Come and join us in the office.' She looked straight at him. 'Mandy has something to tell us, I think,' she said.

Mr Hope looked across at Mandy and raised his eyebrows. Mandy miserably shook her head and plodded into reception, where Simon was standing at Jean's desk, apparently cutting out patterns with her scissors.

'Ah, Mandy!' he said. 'I think we've . . .' He paused as he watched Emily and Adam Hope striding past. Mandy didn't even look up. Only James, catching a glimpse of the papers in Simon's hand, stood back and pushed him on towards the office.

Emily Hope sat alongside her husband behind their desk. 'Do we really need *everyone* here?' she asked Mandy.

Mandy, who felt she needed all the support she could get just then, nodded.

'Right, well, you'd better sit down, then.' She nodded at Simon and James, who squashed down together on the one visitor's chair. Mandy remained where she was, standing in front of the desk, feeling she was about to be interrogated.

But Mrs Hope spoke in a quiet, calm voice. 'Now, Mandy, I think you've a few things to tell us. Like why Mr Bonser caught you up at his farm the other day, for instance.'

So Mandy took a deep breath, threw a desperate glance at her father, and told all. She explained how James and she had gone up to Old Dyke Farm to try to talk to Mr Bonser about the dog. And, she admitted, to take a closer look round his farm.

'It was my fault we went to the farm, Mum, so please don't blame James. He only took the registration number. And Simon's made rubbings of Mr Bonser's tyres today, to check against the plaster casts we made up in the woods. We're going to check on all the local vans if we can.' She paused to glance at her father, who smiled encouragingly.

'But what for, Mandy?' asked her mother.

'Well, if we can stop the badger-digging altogether, Humbug can go back home,' Mandy explained. 'Can't he, James?'

James nodded. 'Walter says there's a chance that the family will come back, if they're left alone,' he said. 'They often move to a kind of sub-sett, then return when they feel it's safe.'

'I can understand that you want to reunite Humbug with his family,' Mrs Hope smiled. 'But I don't see what Mr Bonser has to do with that.'

'Well . . .' Mandy took a deep breath and rushed on. 'I heard dogs whining in the piggeries at Old Dyke Farm. I think Mr Bonser is keeping them half-starved and hungry especially for digging badgers. I think we should do something about it!'

It was so quiet in the crowded office that Mandy could hear her own heart thudding, and James's nervous breathing just behind her.

'Well, you're right about the way he keeps the dogs,' said Mr Hope. 'I wasn't at all happy about the dog's condition when Mr Bonser first brought it in.'

Mrs Hope nodded. 'It wasn't only injured,' she agreed. 'It was half-starved.'

'You see, Mandy, we'd already decided to call in the RSPCA inspector to discuss the matter before contacting Mr Bonser,' Mr Hope explained.

'As it was, Mr Bonser got here first and flew at me!' Even Emily Hope sounded a bit shaken at the memory of her interview with Mr Bonser.

Mandy felt suitably ashamed. 'I'm really sorry, Mum,' she said. 'I never dreamed he'd come over so soon; he didn't seem to care what happened to Patch.'

'Yet he said he needed the dog for something this weekend,' mused Mrs Hope. 'I wonder why?'

'I don't think this has anything to do with protecting his land,' said her husband, grimly. 'I've heard a few rumours on my rounds. I didn't take much notice of them then, just gossip, you know, but Walter Pickard swears something's going on up in the woods this weekend . . .' And he went on to tell them how Walter had heard the men talking about a meeting on Saturday, and something about dogs and a great deal of money.

'I thought they must have been talking about racing greyhounds up at the track in Brudderford,' said Mr Hope. 'But it occurs to me now that it wasn't racing they were discussing at all . . .' He paused and looked round the office. All eyes were on him, James and Mandy looking very puzzled, Mrs Hope and Simon nodding thoughtfully. 'It's much worse than that,' he said.

'I'm afraid they were setting up badger-baiting.'

There was a stunned pause.

'You mean fights?' asked Mandy, in a wobbly voice.

Mr Hope sighed. 'They dig out the badgers, take them off to an old barn somewhere and set their dogs on them. They make bets on which one will win. Ernie Bell tells me it used to be a popular local sport.'

'But surely it's illegal?' said Mrs Hope.

'Of course it's illegal. And cruel. And disgusting.' Mr Hope reached for the telephone. 'And Mandy's right,' he said. 'We've got to do something – and fast!'

Nine

Mandy was not pleased. She'd been all set to dial 999 to get the Walton police station but Mr Hope wouldn't let her. 'Animals first' was his motto; he rang the Walton RSPCA. And now, after all the excitement there was nothing left to do except wait – and watch the rabbits run around the lawn.

Mandy sat on top of the empty hutch, kicking her heels. 'He should have let me ring the police,' she complained. 'What can the RSPCA do about Mr Bonser and his nasty friends?'

'Well, they're used to dealing with animals,' James joked.

But Mandy was in no mood for laughs. 'That's

just it,' she went on. 'They might well rescue the badgers – and the dogs – but in the meantime those . . . those . . . horrible people will be getting away.' Her voice choked. 'We ought to be keeping an eye on them, tracking them down – anything!' Mandy looked around impatiently, as if she'd like to arrest even the rabbits.

'But, Mandy, your dad said they're dangerous men – probably violent!' James shuddered.

He was right and Mandy knew it. Even so, she wished there was someone who would make sure that Mr Bonser and his friends didn't get away. But who?

'Dad said he'd heard rumours about the badger-baiters from Walter Pickard,' she said, thoughtfully.

'Well, Walter always knows what's going on in the woods,' said James. 'That's why he's our secretary.'

'Your secretary?'

'At the Welford Wildlifers,' James explained. 'Mrs Jackson is in charge, but Walter arranges the meetings.'

Mandy suddenly stood up and smiled. 'Well, maybe we'd better pay a visit to our friend Walter,' she said. 'Come on, let's get the rabbits in.'

* * *

'Well, well, if it isn't young James!' Walter was in his garden, sweeping up piles of leaves. 'And young miss with you, as well. New member is she?'

Blushing furiously, James shook his head.

'We just came to talk to you, Mr Pickard,' Mandy explained.

The big man pushed back his flat cap and peered down at Mandy and James. 'What can I do for you?' he asked.

'Well . . .' Mandy looked over her shoulder towards the garden gate. 'May we sit on your bench?' she asked. No point in the whole street hearing.

'Aye – come along with me, it's warm enough to sit out today.' Walter led the way and the three of them squashed together on the bench by the back door. As soon as they were settled, Walter's three cats came out to sit in the pale, autumn sunshine with them. Mandy bent to stroke Scraps whilst she collected her thoughts.

'Mr Pickard,' she began, 'Dad said you'd heard rumours about something going on up in the woods.'

Walter sucked at his teeth and nodded. 'I have that, young miss,' he said, in his deep, Yorkshire voice. 'Up to no good, somebody is up there.'

'Do you know who?' asked James.

Walter looked sideways at them. 'It's not for me to say,' he said, cautiously. 'But I have my suspicions. I have that!'

Mandy looked at James. James looked at Mandy. This was going to be difficult; they didn't want to give away all their evidence to Walter, who loved a good gossip. On the other hand, they did want to arouse his interest.

'You know Humbug, the baby badger that James rescued from Piper's Wood?' Mandy began.

The old man nodded. 'Oh, aye,' he said. 'Keeping all right, is he?' He turned to James.

'Yes, he's all right,' James picked up Mandy's train of thought. 'But it's getting time to set him free again. You warned me that we couldn't keep him away from the sett for more than a week or two.'

'That's right, young James. I'm glad you're keeping that in mind.' Walter gazed up the garden path and nodded slowly. 'I'm reminded of that time when I were a lad. Ernie Bell – just a lad himself – brought a badger out. Reared it like a ferret, he did, in a cage at the bottom of their garden. But he kept it too long. It got that big!'

Walter stretched out his hands. 'Solid an' all, it were. We didn't know what to do with it . . .'

'That's just it, you see,' Mandy burst in. 'If we turn Humbug – that baby badger – loose, and the diggers are still around . . .'

'Aye. And more than diggers, I hear.' Walter's eyes gleamed.

'Well, what we were wondering . . . my dad's got the RSPCA inspector coming round this afternoon and we've got to be there to tell him about . . . about how we found the badger. But we heard there's going to be more digging and we think somebody ought to keep an eye . . .'

'Certainly!' Walter drew himself up. 'This is a job for the Wildlife Watch Committee. Mrs Jackson's away just now, but I'll go up to the post office and talk to McFarlane. We often take a walk up the woods of an afternoon. Don't you worry, youngsters, we'll keep our eyes open.'

'Oh, thank you, Mr Pickard.' Mandy beamed up at him.

'It's nothing, lass,' said the old man, standing stiff, but tall and upright on his garden path. 'I'd best be getting off to see McFarlane, then . . .'

'Yes and we'd best be getting off back to Animal Ark.' James nudged Mandy and they both stood up. 'Thanks again, Mr Pickard!'

Together they raced back up the village, past the
Fox and Goose and along the lane to Animal
Ark. Mandy turned in at the gate first, then
stopped.

'Wait!' she commanded. 'Look at that!'

She pointed to the front of the house where her
father was leaning casually against the Land-rover
and chatting to a tall, red-faced man with a dark
beard.

Mandy pulled James into the rhododendrons.
'That's him!' she hissed.

'Who?' he asked, peering out of the bushes.

'Get back!' Mandy urged him. 'Isn't that the man
who was spying on us in the woods? You know,
the day you made the plaster casts.'

'I don't know; I didn't see him.'

They crouched together in the bushes, peering
down the path to the carpark.

'I'm sure that's him,' said Mandy. 'And he was
curious to know what you were doing that day.'

'Well, I expect it did look a bit odd,' said James.

'Yes, but he seemed to be checking up on us,'
Mandy replied. 'Blackie even growled at him.'

'Just protecting you, I expect,' smiled James.

'Yes,' said Mandy. 'Blackie knew he was up to no good.' She pushed the fronds of leaves aside to clear her view. 'I don't like it,' she said. 'He's talking to my dad.'

'He looks quite friendly,' observed James. 'Maybe he's a friend of your dad's.'

Mandy threw him a withering glance. 'A friend of Mr Bonser's, more like,' she said. 'He's just come to spy on us, or to pinch the evidence or . . .'

'Or to get the dog?' suggested James.

Mandy stared at him. 'You're right,' she said. 'Mr Bonser's sent him to get his dog – maybe even to pay his bill. And you know what Dad is . . .'

James smiled. He did know. Mr Hope was wonderful with animals but soft as a brush with people. When it came to dealing with Mr Bonser's lot he wouldn't stand a chance.

'And Mum's out on a farm call,' groaned Mandy. 'Come on, we'd better rescue Dad!'

They rushed down the drive but as they approached the house, they walked slowly, trying to look casual.

'Where on earth have you two been?' said Adam Hope. 'This gentleman's waiting to see you. And he's been telling me all kinds of interesting things about our Mr Bonser.'

'I'll bet he has,' Mandy whispered. 'Like how he loves dogs and protects badgers.' She nudged James forward and followed, slowly.

'Come on!' Mr Hope urged. 'Now then, Ted, this is my daughter, Mandy, and James Hunter, a friend of hers.' He beamed down at the two of them. Neither looked at the stranger.

'This is Mr Forrester,' Adam Hope went on. 'Our new RSPCA inspector from Walton.'

There was a pause. Mandy opened her mouth, but nothing came out.

'I think we've met, haven't we, Mandy?' Mr Forrester smiled. 'Up in Piper's Wood, a few days ago?'

Mandy merely nodded.

'I hear you did a good job up there,' the inspector went on, turning to James. 'And the badger's doing well?'

'I hope so,' said James. 'But I want to return him to the sett as soon as . . . as it's safe.'

Mr Forrester nodded. 'Well, from what I've seen, we should be able to make it safe, for your badger and for any others which come back.'

James's eyes lit up. 'You think they might come back?' he asked.

'I think they already have done,' said the

inspector. 'I've been keeping a careful watch on the sett, as you know.' He looked sideways at Mandy, who blushed. 'There are traces – tracks and droppings, but no sign of them having settled in yet.'

'But you think they will?' asked Mr Hope.

'If they're left in peace.'

Mandy suddenly woke up. 'Well, they won't be left in peace unless we do something about Mr Bonser,' she pointed out.

Mr Forrester smiled at her. 'You're right,' he said. 'So shall we go in now and examine the evidence?' He looked at Mr Hope.

'Yes, yes, of course.' Mr Hope searched all his pockets for the surgery keys and looked vaguely all round. 'Now, where . . . ?'

Mandy reached into the car, fished a set of keys from the glove compartment and handed them to her father.

'Thank you. Right then, off we go!' Mr Hope led the way, James followed, then Mr Forrester, and, last of all, very quiet and thoughtful, came Mandy.

'These are very good casts,' said Mr Forrester, holding them up and examining them carefully.

'Lucky I saw you making them that day, isn't it?'

'Why?' asked James.

'Well, our friend Bonser could always claim you took the casts some other time,' said Mr Forrester. 'It's always useful to have an official witness.'

James looked knowingly over his glasses at Mandy. Mandy nodded and smiled back at him. Well, James had been right about Mr Forrester after all! They both watched the inspector pick up the photographs of the injured terrier. He looked at them in surprise.

'Good heavens!' he exclaimed.

'She was in a mess,' Adam Hope agreed. 'You

can see how talk started about some wild cat up there.'

Mr Forrester went on looking closely at the photographs, nodding thoughtfully. 'I'd like to see this dog right now, if you wouldn't mind.'

'Of course! Mandy will take you up there. And I'll ring that wildlife officer at police headquarters. Sergeant Wilkins, you said his name was?'

Mr Forrester nodded. 'Walton 78357, that'll get you straight through to him.' He turned. 'Now then, Mandy, let's go and look at this dog, shall we?'

Mandy walked beside Mr Forrester with very mixed feelings. She felt foolish for having mistaken him for one of Mr Bonser's men but relieved that at last he was getting things moving. And then she felt worried for Patch. Why was the inspector so interested in the little dog? Was he going to punish her for digging out badgers?

Silently she clicked open the cage and called, 'Patch? Come on, girl, come to me.'

The little dog put her head out cautiously, sniffed the air and hobbled out towards Mandy.

'Paddy!' Mr Forrester suddenly spoke. 'It *is* you – I thought it was! Come on, Paddy, here lass.'

The dog hesitated, looking first at Mandy then

at Mr Forrester. Mandy glared at the man; what did he mean by calling the dog Paddy? Suddenly, as if finally making up her mind, the little dog trotted up to Mr Forrester, yelping happily, jumping up and pawing his trousers. Mr Forrester bent down and picked her up.

'Well, I'm blowed!' he said, beaming across at Mandy. 'I never thought to see this little tyke again.'

Mandy just stood, staring, thoughts whirling round her head. 'Paddy', not 'Patch'. And the dog had chosen to run to Mr Forrester, not her. But how on earth did Patch know him?

The dog was wriggling in the man's arms, nuzzling up to his shoulder and whimpering with joy. For a moment, Mandy felt jealous; but even she couldn't help smiling at the little dog's delight.

'You know her, then?' she asked.

Mr Forrester pushed the dog's nose away from his face and nodded. 'I should say so! She's Jess Hargreaves's new farm dog. He took her from our dogs' home a few months ago when she turned up as a stray. When the dog went missing, I thought she'd run back to wherever she'd come from, but Jess was convinced she'd been stolen.'

'Well, he was right,' Mandy pointed out.

'Aye, he was that.' Mr Forrester looked grimly down at the dog. 'And when we catch up with that Bonser, I'll remember Jess's face, the night his Paddy never came home.' He sighed and hugged the dog close.

Mandy stood watching, feeling rather awkward. Another case of mistaken identity, she thought. Well, at least Paddy didn't belong to Mr Bonser. Mandy knew that Jess Hargreaves took good care of all the animals on his farm.

Mr Forrester put the dog down and she ran up to Mandy, who knelt down and fussed her.

'You'll not want to see her go,' observed Mr Forrester.

Mandy blushed. 'Well, so long as she's not going back to that Mr Bonser,' she said.

'No, she's going back where she belongs – to work on a farm. You should see her snapping and nipping at those cows; gets them to the milking parlour in record time, she does!'

'I can just imagine her doing a job like that,' smiled Mandy. And she told Mr Forrester how Paddy had sniffed out Humbug in the basement.

He laughed. 'Well, Jess will be that thrilled to get her back,' he said. 'I must ring him right away.'

'Come on back to the office,' said Mandy. 'You can use the phone there.' Together they put Paddy into her hut and left her to sleep off her excitement, whilst they went off to face theirs.

Sergeant Wilkins, Mr Forrester and Mr Hope sat in the office, talking about Wildlife Acts and Cruelty to Animals Acts as if they had months to spare. Mandy was bursting to hear their plans, but she and James were dispatched to the kitchen with Mrs Hope and a policewoman to make their statements.

The policewoman made it all quite easy for them. She didn't ask them questions, but just let them tell her everything, right from the beginning, into a tape recorder.

'May I go back, now?' asked James.

The policewoman nodded. 'Want a lift home?' she offered.

'No thanks, I have to see to Humbug first,' said James.

'Ah, yes, the badger you rescued. Mind if I come and look at him?'

James looked doubtful. 'He's had rather a disturbing day,' he said.

'Oh, I'll be very quiet,' she assured him. 'I've

been a badger watcher for years. Do you have a badger watch in Welford?'

'No, but we could start one with the Wildlifers.' James smiled happily, and led her off, chatting all the time about badger problems. Mandy silently watched them go across the garden to the path to Lilac Cottage.

'Aren't you going with them?' asked her mother.

Mandy tossed her head and sniffed.

'What's the point in taking care of Humbug?' she asked. 'At this rate, there won't be anywhere safe for him to go back to!'

'What do you mean?'

'Well, there's Dad and the others all chatting away in the office, and James and that policewoman chatting away in the garden, and nobody's doing anything about catching Mr Bonser.' Mandy was impatient to get something done.

Her mother sat down next to her and put an arm round her. 'Don't be so impatient, Mandy,' she said. 'The police and the RSPCA are planning to catch Bonser red-handed tonight.'

'Tonight?' repeated Mandy, dismayed. 'But why leave it till then? Why don't they just go and arrest them right now?'

Mrs Hope shook her head. 'They've got to catch them at it,' she explained. 'Remember what Walter overheard? The next badger-digging will be this evening up in Darley Woods. And that's where they'll be caught.'

Mandy sniffed. 'But what about "animals first"?' she asked. 'We can't risk another injured dog, or badger even.'

'And we won't,' her mother promised. 'The police and the RSPCA inspectors will pounce before the dogs are even loose. There'll be no badger-baiting tonight.'

'Only Bonser-baiting?' Mandy smiled a wobbly smile.

Mrs Hope smiled back. 'That's right, Mandy,' she said. 'Now, how about taking some tea into the centre of operations?'

Ten

'It's not fair!' Mandy said to James as they went off to feed Humbug.

It had never occurred to her that she wouldn't be there to see Mr Bonser arrested. But Dad was quite firm; he would go along to check the dogs; the police and Ted Forrester's RSPCA team would do the rest. Children were not allowed!

'But we did all the work!' she said. 'We collected all the evidence, and now they won't even let us watch them catch him! Typical!' She slammed a tin of vitamin mixture down on the shelf.

'Shh!' James warned her.

He needn't have bothered. Stirred by Mandy's

voice, Humbug stretched up at the bars of his cage and snuffled hopefully.

'See, he knows you now,' said James.

Mandy forgot her bad temper and pushed a finger through to stroke the badger's nose. Assuming it was food, Humbug tried to suck on it.

'Ow!' cried Mandy. 'He may know my voice, but he doesn't know a finger from a pellet!'

James laughed. 'We've got to take him back to the sett once Mr Bonser's safely out of the way,' he said.

Mandy said nothing. Suddenly she felt quite left out; there was nothing for her to do. Not only was she going to miss all the action up in Darley Woods tonight, but she'd lost Patch! As soon as Jess Hargreaves had heard the news he'd come straight down to Animal Ark to collect his dog.

Sighing, she pressed the plastic lid on Humbug's pellet box and wandered back across the garden to Animal Ark. There was nothing much to look forward to now except school, she thought.

At six o'clock that evening, Adam Hope drove off in the Land-rover up to Darley Woods, to meet Ted Forrester, Sergeant Wilkins and their wildlife teams.

'Everybody's going to be there except me,' Mandy grumbled to her mother.

'And me,' Mrs Hope smiled. 'Shall we have supper on a tray in front of the television?' she offered.

Mandy knew she was giving her a treat, to make up for missing all the excitement – and to keep her occupied until they got some news. 'Thanks, Mum, what shall we have?' she said.

'I thought we'd share a pizza.'

'Great! And I'll mix the salad.' Mandy rushed off to the kitchen, relieved to have something to do to pass the time until her father came home.

But during supper, she couldn't relax. She hardly noticed what was on television, and only nibbled at her pizza.

'Come on, Mandy, it's no use worrying. Dad'll be all right,' said her mother.

'I know he will.' Mandy suddenly felt rather ashamed; she hadn't even been worrying about her father. 'I'm just sorry I won't be there to see it all through to the end.'

'I know, love, but these are dangerous men. You couldn't do anything even if you were there.'

'I could watch from a distance, couldn't I?'

Emily Hope looked at her daughter's sad face

and smiled. 'Honestly, darling, don't you think they'll have enough to do without looking after you?'

'I wouldn't need looking after,' Mandy assured her.

'No, perhaps not,' her mother agreed. 'But Dad'll be able to concentrate better without you there.'

And Mandy had to agree with that. She turned her attention to the hospital series on television and was soon engrossed.

She was so gripped by the programme that she didn't even hear the doorbell. Mum went off to answer it and came back with a worried-looking Walter Pickard.

' . . . so you see, missus, I thought I should come and tell Mr Hope 'cause he'd know what to do.'

Mandy turned off the television and looked at Walter's worried face. In spite of the blazing fire at her back, she suddenly felt cold.

'What is it?' she asked. 'Did you see something in the woods this afternoon?'

The old man shook his head. 'No, nothing happening up there today,' he said. 'Except we found traces of the badgers. I think they'll be ready to come back to their sett any time now if they're left in peace.' He turned to Mrs Hope. 'Then, Ernie Bell and me, we always goes for a game of dominoes at the Fox and Goose, early on, like. Good drop of ale they keeps there.'

'Yes, so I hear,' Mrs Hope smiled.

'But what has that to do with badgers?' asked Mandy, impatiently.

'What? Oh, aye. Well, it was very quiet about then, d'you see? And Ernie, well, takes a month of Sundays to decide which domino to play. So I'm just sitting there, waiting and sipping and . . . well . . . hearing . . .' Walter hesitated.

'And what did you hear?' Emily Hope prompted.

'It was from across t'other bar, you see? Two voices – sounded foreign to me . . .'

'Foreign?' Mandy asked, surprised.

'Aye, Lancashire maybe – or even up the Lakes somewhere. Anyway, they were talking about dogs and money and grumbling away about some meeting being changed . . .'

'Changed?' Mrs Hope's voice was suddenly anxious.

He nodded. 'Aye, changed from Darley Woods one chap said. Then the other asked him if he'd got a map, and first one said he didn't need it, he'd been up Piper's Wood before . . .'

'Piper's Wood!' both Mandy and her mother exclaimed.

'Aye, said as how they'd all meet up there . . .'

'When?' asked Mrs Hope, sharply.

Walter shrugged. 'I dunno,' he said. 'Ernie put his domino down just then and by the time I'd played him out they'd gone.'

'But you think they meant tonight?'

'Certain sure. That's why I wanted to tell Mr Hope, you see? Young James told me he was seeing the RSPCA chap and I thought . . .'

'Yes, yes, you were quite right, but they've all gone off to Darley Woods! Oh, what on earth should we do?' Emily Hope stood up and paced round the sitting-room, biting her lip anxiously.

Mandy stood up, too. 'We'll have to get a message over to them,' she cried. 'Let's call the police.'

That was only the start of Mandy's surprising evening. As soon as she'd passed the message on to the police station at Walton she rang James and told him to get ready for a badger watch.

'A what?' James couldn't believe his luck.

'Well, it's a Bonser watch really.' Mandy explained that Walter and her mum were going to keep an eye on things until the official party arrived. 'And I've persuaded Mum to let me come along this time. You will come, won't you?'

James hesitated. Watching badgers was one thing, but getting involved with Bonser and his crew . . . 'I don't know if they'll let me,' he said.

'Of course they will if you tell them you're with Mum. See you in ten minutes – be ready!' Mandy put down the phone and, smiling happily to herself, went in search of wellingtons.

'And you're to stay in the car no matter what happens, do you hear?' Mrs Hope told Mandy and

James. 'Walter and I will keep watch in the undergrowth closer to the sett. You lock the car and stay there. Right?'

'Right, Mum,' Mandy promised.

It was already quite dark in the woods but Mrs Hope didn't want to use the lights. Slowly, cautiously, she drove the car along the track where Mandy had found the tyre prints that day. It seemed like months ago, she realised now. But before she could comment, the two adults were out of the car and checking the doors.

'We're only keeping watch until the others arrive,' said Mum. 'Chances are, nothing will happen this part of the evening.'

'I hope she's wrong,' said Mandy. 'Don't you?'

'Hmm.' James didn't sound very sure.

He'd rather be watching for badgers than for badger-baiters, Mandy reflected. She waved to Walter, who gave a thumbs-up sign and followed Mrs Hope into the undergrowth.

And then it was very, very quiet. Mandy would never admit it, but she actually slept for a while. She was awakened by James gripping her arm.

'Look!' he whispered pointing across the clearing.

Mandy saw lights – torches – and heard people

pushing through the undergrowth. Then the sound of panting, snuffling, the occasional yelp. The dogs!

'What shall we do?' she whispered.

'Nothing – just watch,' said James.

'We'll get a better view at the front,' suggested Mandy.

She and James clambered into the front seats, watching the procession as it made its way to the clearing. The car was well hidden but even so, Mandy felt a shiver run right through her. Where was her mother? And Walter? And, more important, had Dad and the others got the message?

Pushing her worries away, Mandy concentrated on the scene before her. Several men now appeared in the lamplight, carrying ropes, spades, and some smaller tools Mandy didn't recognise. The dogs strained and tugged on the bits of rope that held them, sniffing and yelping, pulling the men closer and closer to the sett.

'I hope they don't get the scent of Walter or Mum,' whispered Mandy.

'Not Walter; he'll have the sense to stay upwind of them and your mum'll be with him.'

Just then a terrible sound hit the air. A scream,

a shriek, and a long, high howl that ended in a series of agonised yelps.

Mandy sat up still and straight. 'What's that?' she whispered.

James pushed his glasses up his nose and peered through the front window. 'I can't see,' he moaned. 'It's all misted up.'

'Wipe the windows – come on!' Mandy started rubbing at hers with her handkerchief.

James hesitated. 'I haven't got a hankie,' he said.

'Well, look in the glove compartment – there's usually a duster or something in there.'

James found the duster and wiped his window down then stood up to clean the whole of the front while Mandy peered out. In the bobbing lamp-light she could just make out a circle of figures – the badger-baiters. Within the circle she saw two short, dark shadows shifting about each other then, suddenly, launching one on top of the other. And the screaming and the shrieking again.

Sickened, Mandy sank back in her seat. 'What shall we do? What shall we do?' she moaned, her face hidden in her hands.

James joined her; she could feel him trembling even through the car seat. 'They didn't even have to dig one out tonight,' he said, bitterly. 'That was probably Humbug's mother coming to look for him again.'

For a moment both of them sat, silent, shaking, looking nowhere, at nothing. Then suddenly the car was flooded with light.

'What's that?' Mandy lifted up her face and saw a dazzling light that filled the clearing. People were racing across the grass right into the circle of badger-baiters. Then howls and barks and thuds and curses.

Mandy and James stood up now and leaned forwards to the front window, trying to make sense of the scene. Police were certainly there – and Dad! Mandy could see his heavy figure crouched down by the pack of dogs and she knew he would be muzzling them.

As she strained forward to see more clearly, Mandy saw a figure pounding along the track towards them. One of them had got away! She cowered back as the figure hesitated in front of the car. What if he tried to get in? Mandy watched fearfully as he pushed past and pounded off down the bridle-path.

Then, something hit the roof with a clang. Mandy jumped, still afraid that someone might be trying to get in. But whatever it was slid down the back of the car and all was quiet again.

'What was that?' James jumped. He hadn't even seen the escaped man. 'It sounded as if somebody threw something at us,' he said.

That was it! Mandy realised. The man had thrown something over his shoulder as he ran away. But what could it have been? And whatever it was, he was keen to lose it.

She turned to tell James about him, but he was peering through the front window again.

'Here's your mum and Walter,' he said. 'It's all over.'

'You all right, you two?' Mrs Hope unlocked the front doors. 'See, you didn't miss out after all.' She smiled at the two of them, sitting quietly in the front seats. 'Hop into the back, then.'

As they scrambled out of the front of the car, Mandy nipped to the back. She could see nothing in the dark, but she caught the toe of her trainer on something hard. She bent down and picked up some sort of metal tool. It felt long and thin and swung in her hand, as if on a pivot. What on earth could it be?

'Come on, Mandy – get in quickly!' her mother urged her.

Shoving the tool up into her anorak sleeve, Mandy joined James in the back seat.

'Don't forget your belts,' Mrs Hope warned them.

Mandy groped around for her seat-belt. As her fingers connected with the metal buckle, she wondered just what she'd got up her sleeve. She was about to bring it out and tell them all about it but everyone else was busy talking.

'Was the badger hurt?' James was asking.

'Good heavens, no,' Mrs Hope reassured him. 'She was a real fighter. Now we know where Paddy got those wounds.'

Mandy remembered her first sight of the little terrier and shuddered. So her wounds could have been caused by one of Humbug's own family! 'What about the dog?' she asked.

'Mr Hope's bringing it back,' said Walter. 'The others are going to the dogs' home. They're a right wild pack and no mistake.'

'And the men?' asked James. 'What will happen to them?' Mandy knew he was hoping that Mr Bonser would be put out of the way so that Humbug could return to the sett.

But her mother didn't answer straight away.

'Well, they'll be charged, of course,' she said,

slowly. 'Probably for ill-treating the dogs, not the badgers. Trouble is, they claim they were digging out foxes. Mr Bonser says he hired them because the foxes have been at his poultry. Fox-digging has only recently been made illegal – everybody knows it still goes on.'

'Aye,' Walter went on. 'And everybody who's lost any chickens to a fox will agree with Bonser.'

'But surely no one will believe they were after foxes?' asked Mandy.

'What they believe and what they can prove are two different things,' said Walter. 'That's what they need – some real hard evidence.'

Mandy sat in the back of the car, feeling her arm stiff where the metal was still hidden up her sleeve. Was this 'real, hard evidence'? It felt a bit long and thin, with rounded bits that got caught in the lining of her sleeve. Well, it might be important, she thought. After all, that man had tried to get rid of it. But how could a bit of metal turn into crucial evidence? Mandy's thoughts whirled but she was too tired to make any sense of them just then.

I'll wait till Dad gets home, she promised herself. *He'll know what it's all about.* She yawned, put her head back on the seat and was almost asleep by the time they arrived at Animal Ark.

Eleven

It was just like a party in the kitchen at Animal Ark. Walter sat by the cooker drinking coffee with Ted Forrester, Mr and Mrs Hunter called to collect James and stayed on to hear all about the night's events, Adam Hope poured drinks and Emily Hope made a stack of sandwiches for everyone.

'Well, let's hope those men get put away for a very long time,' said Mrs Hunter.

'Oh, they'll claim they were only after foxes,' said Mr Hope, handing her a drink. 'They'll probably get away with a fine for that.'

'And they'll still be free to dig out our badgers!'

said Mrs Hunter. 'We'll have to keep a look out from now on.'

'You'd be at it twenty-four hours a day,' said Ted Forrester. 'And even then they'd find another sett in some other wood.'

Walter nodded in agreement. 'McFarlane's trying to get a badgerwatch started,' he said. 'But there's not enough Wildlifers to keep watch round the clock.'

Mandy put down her glass of Coke and looked across the table at James. He pushed a sandwich round his plate, making no attempt to eat it. She knew he was thinking about Humbug, worrying about setting him free with the baiters still on the loose . . .

'Well, the police will comb that clearing tomorrow,' Mr Hope was telling Mrs Hunter. 'They must have got rid of at least one pair of tongs.'

'Tongs? What do they use them for?' asked Mrs Hunter.

And across the table, Mandy was all ears.

'They use them to lift the badgers,' Adam Hope explained. 'To avoid those strong claws, you see.'

'And they'd only need them if they were after badgers, not foxes?' Mandy asked.

'Well, yes – they're a dead giveaway,' her father told her. 'But those men certainly hadn't got any with them tonight.'

'Oh, yes, they had,' said Mandy. 'Hang on!' She ran out to the hall and came back struggling with her anorak.

'What on earth . . . ?' asked Emily Hope. 'Do be careful, Mandy – you'll tear that sleeve.'

'There you are!' Mandy finally extricated the metal tongs from her anorak. She held them up for everyone to see. 'A man ran past our car while you and the police were all busy,' she explained. 'And he threw these behind him.'

'How did you find them?' asked Mrs Hope.

'I heard them clatter on the car roof and slide down the back,' said Mandy.

'That's right,' said James. 'We wondered what it was.'

'Then, when we got out of the car to change places,' Mandy explained, 'I looked round the back and just about fell over these things.'

'Well done, Mandy,' said Ted Forrester. 'Tongs are always accepted as vital evidence.'

'But what if the gang deny they were theirs?' asked Mr Hunter. 'Mandy's fingerprints must be all over them by now.'

Mandy looked round in dismay. After all that, she hadn't got any real, hard evidence! If only she'd left them for the police to pick up!

'Don't worry, Mandy,' her father reassured her. 'If the runaway man had any sense he'd already wiped them clean.'

Mandy smiled – a small, wan smile. She still felt disappointed that her evidence was not going to be as final as she'd hoped.

But Walter Pickard was speaking. 'Well, I'll bet them there tongs have got some mark or other on them, Mr Hope,' he said.

'What do you mean?'

'Well, country folk generally mark their tools, so that when other folk borrows 'em and never bring 'em back, they can prove who they belong to, see?'

'You mean the tongs will have a name on them?' Mandy asked.

'Nay, it won't be a name. More a sign, like.' Walter fiddled in his waistcoat pocket and brought out a pair of round, steel-rimmed glasses. 'Now, give them tongs to me,' he said to Mandy. 'Careful, now . . .' He took the tongs by one of the handles, holding it delicately in his broad fingers, and peered closely at the blades.

Everyone watched. No one spoke. The tongs spun round, catching the light. Suddenly Walter pointed to a mark scratched deep into the metal right on the joint of the two blades.

'Reckon that's a "B",' he said. 'You mark my words!'

Ted Forrester passed extra-strong peppermints to the other two with him in the hide. 'To keep you awake,' he said. 'I always use them when I'm keeping watch.'

'For badgers or criminals?' asked Mandy.

'Both,' he grinned.

'Shh!' said James, anxiously peering through the hide he and Walter had made earlier that day, before they set Humbug free.

Now it was nightfall and Ted Forrester had brought them on the first badger watch of the season. Mandy had never been keen on just watching animals; she preferred to be close enough to touch them. But now she was really excited. She sucked so hard on her mint that her eyes began to water. She shook her head and looked out into the moonlight to clear them. And as she peered out, she caught sight of a movement in the deep shadows under the trees. She peered

more closely and saw it emerge into the moonlight
– a badger.

But it wasn't Humbug. It was a larger, older
animal which trotted out into the clearing so
quickly that Mandy thought perhaps it was merely
a shadow, a trick of the light.

But Ted had seen it too. 'A fully-grown male,'
he whispered. 'See the length of him? And how
black the markings are on his face? Females are
lighter – in weight as well as colour; fatter, too.'

Mandy and James followed his gaze. The badger
was certainly bigger than Mandy had ever
imagined. He trotted out into the clearing, lifted
up his dark snout and sniffed. They could even
hear him!

'Now, don't get too excited; they often live alone,
male badgers.'

Suddenly the badger stopped, sat down, and
began to have a good scratch. Mandy could hear
the rasping of his claws quite clearly, could see
the sharp snout, lifted into the light. She felt a
shiver of excitement; her first really wild badger!
Even if Ted Forrester was right, and this was a
solitary male, it was worth waiting for.

But Ted was wrong. As the first badger sat
enjoying his scratch, another smaller but plumper

animal emerged into the light, closely pursued by two cubs!

'Young female – and cubs!' James sounded excited even in whispers.

Mandy held her breath. Was one of them Humbug?

But there was too much going on to worry about Humbug. First the male stopped scratching, sat up, and gently rolled the cubs around on the grass. Then he lay down and allowed the cubs to 'attack' him. It was so quiet that the badger watchers could hear the excited squeaks of the cubs as they rolled all over the male, and fell off his back, into the grass.

Suddenly, the female darted forward, grabbed a cub in both of her front paws, and began to groom it roughly, pushing and licking and patting it into shape. Satisfied, she let him go back to his game and grabbed the other one. This time she was gentler, coaxing, rather than forcing the little creature to stay still, licking him delicately, lovingly.

'That's Humbug!' breathed Mandy. 'She's being extra careful with him because she lost him once.'

'Might very well be,' Ted Forrester nodded. 'She's certainly taking extra care of that little 'un. I don't think we need to worry about Humbug any more,' said Ted Forrester. 'He's been accepted, all right.'

As if to prove him right, the smallest badger ran off squeaking into the shadows, pursued by the other cub and their mother. The male snuffled around in the grass, making his way into the undergrowth, slowly, steadily, and then he was gone.

So was the light; clouds covered the moon and the woods were suddenly quite dark.

'Time to go home, I think,' said Ted. And the three of them wriggled out of the hide, through the bracken, and ran down the track to his car.

'Brilliant!' declared Mandy from the back seat. 'That was one of my best nights ever.'

'Better than looking after sick animals even?' inquired James.

Mandy laughed. 'Of course it was,' she said. Better than checking the animals of Animal Ark or playing with her pet rabbit, she thought. Perhaps when she grew up she'd be a Wildlife Officer like Sergeant Wilkins, or an RSPCA inspector like Ted.

Mandy gazed dreamily into the gathering darkness until she saw the words 'Animal Ark' picked out by the headlights. She smiled. Perhaps she'd be a vet after all.

Dear Reader

I'm so pleased with the letters I have been receiving about Animal Ark. *It seems there are a great number of fans of the series, and I am very happy that so many people are enjoying the books.*

I especially enjoy reading your suggestions for new titles – so keep them coming!

Much love

Lucy Daniels

h HODDER *Another Hodder Children's Book*

Lucy Daniels

CUB IN THE CUPBOARD

Mandy and James are horrified when they discover a mother fox caught in a cruel trap – so is the rest of Welford! But somebody local must be responsible . . .

The two friends are determined to find the culprit. But first, who can look after the mischievous fox cub?

Lucy Daniels

PIGLET IN A PLAYPEN

Ruby the piglet is the runt of the litter and there is no place for her on Greystones Farm. But she's cheeky and adventurous, and she's won the hearts of Mandy and James – they can't accept that Ruby has to go.

Can Mandy and James turn the under-sized piglet into a prize-winning pig?

h HODDER

Another Hodder Children's Book

Lucy Daniels

OWL IN THE OFFICE

Mandy has rescued all kinds of animals, but now she faces her toughest challenge yet! Sam Western has put up the local animal shelter's rent. It will have to close – but what will happen to all the animals?

Can Mandy raise the money needed to save the animal shelter?

Lucy Daniels

LAMB IN THE LAUNDRY

Mandy and James discover a tiny black lamb that's been abandoned by its mother. But just when they start to take care of it, the lamb disappears.

Can they find the little lamb before it's too late?